# BOSTON RED SOX

## YESTERDAY & TODAY ™

Nick Carfardo

Publications International, Ltd.

**Nick Cafardo** has covered Boston sports since 1975 and the Boston Red Sox for *The Quincy Patriot-Ledger* and *The Boston Globe* since 1983. He has served as the New England Patriots beat writer for *The Boston Globe* for three Super Bowl championships and four Super Bowl appearances. He has authored two books: *None but the Braves* with Tom Glavine and *The Impossible Team*, the story of the Patriots' first Super Bowl championship. He currently serves as *The Boston Globe* national baseball writer. Cafardo, a New England native, was born in Plymouth, Massachusetts. He and his wife, Leeanne, have two children, Ben and Emilee.

*Pictured on the front cover, clockwise from top left:* David Ortiz launches one against the Yankees; Ted Williams, one of Boston's most-feared sluggers; Dustin Pedroia, Matt Clement, and Doug Mirabelli celebrate the club's four-game World Series sweep over the Rockies in 2007; (from left to right) Ted Williams, Mel Parnell, and Johnny Pesky.

*Pictured on the back cover, from left to right:* Jim Lonborg faces off against the Cardinals in Game 2 of the World Series in 1967; Jon Lester comes through in Game 4 of the World Series against the Rockies in 2007.

Yesterday & Today is a trademark of Publications International, Ltd.

Louis Weber, CEO
Publications International, Ltd.
7373 North Cicero Avenue
Lincolnwood, Illinois 60712

Permission is never granted for commercial purposes.

ISBN-13: 978-1-4127-7906-7
ISBN-10: 1-4127-7906-5

Manufactured in China.

8 7 6 5 4 3 2 1

Library of Congress Control Number: 2009923737

Picture Credits:

Front cover: © **Corbis** Bettmann (top right & bottom left); Rick Friedman (top left); **Getty Images** (bottom right)

Back cover: **AP Images** (left); *Sports Illustrated*/**Getty Images** (right)

**AP Images:** 6, 10 (bottom), 14, 20, 24 (right), 33 (top left), 36 (top), 37 (left), 39 (bottom), 41 (top), 45, 49 (left), 50, 51 (top), 53, 77, 80, 81 (bottom), 82 (right), 83, 84 (top), 85, 86 (top), 87, 88 (left), 89, 103, 106, 107 (left), 109 (right), 111, 113, 118, 119, 121, 124 (top), 126 (top), 131, 133 (right), 135, 137 (right), 138, 139 (left); **Getty Images:** 7, 11, 12, 13 (top), 16 (top), 17, 19, 21 (left), 25, 30, 32 (right), 40 (top), 46 (bottom), 91 (center), 94 (top), 95 (top left), 100 (top left), 114 (right), 115, 129 (top), 130 (left), 132, 136, 140, 142 (bottom), 143; Christian Science Monitor, 28 (left); Diamond Images, 98 (left), 112 (bottom); Focus on Sports, 59 (top), 101, 104, 105, 127; MLB Photos, 29, 48, 64 (top), 73, 74, 78, 97, 141 (top); **Index Stock Imagery, Inc.:** Tom Hannon, 18 (bottom), **PIL Collection:** 8, 9, 10, 13 (bottom), 15 (bottom), 16 (bottom), 18, 21 (right), 23, 24 (left), 26 (center), 28, 29, 31, 32 (left), 33, 34, 35, 38, 39 (top & center), 40 (bottom), 41 (bottom), 42, 43, 44 (top & bottom), 46 (top), 47, 51 (bottom), 52, 54, 56 (left), 57, 58, 60, 62, 63, 64 (center), 65, 66, 67, 68, 69, 70, 71, 72, 73, 75, 76, 77, 79, 81 (top), 82 (center), 84 (bottom), 86 (right), 88 (right), 90, 91 (top), 92 (center), 93, 94 (bottom), 95 (top center & bottom left), 96, 98 (right), 99, 100 (right & bottom left), 102, 104, 107 (right), 108, 109 (left), 110, 112 (right center), 114 (left), 116, 117, 119, 120, 122, 123 (bottom), 124 (bottom), 125, 126 (bottom), 128, 129 (bottom), 130 (right), 133 (left), 134, 137 (left), 139 (right), 141 (bottom), 142 (top); **Shutterstock:** 15 (top), 22; **SuperStock:** age fotostock, 26 (top), 27, 31; Transcendental Graphics: Dick Dobbins Collection, 37 (right); Mark Rucker, 36 (bottom), 44 (top right), 55, 59 (bottom), 92 (top); Mark Rucker/M. Brown, 33 (top right); Mark Rucker/Felder, 56 (right); **Jerry Yamamoto Collection:** 49 (right), 123 (top)

The grounds crew prepares the field for a game at Fenway Park on September 16, 2004. A rainbow appears in the sky, possibly a sign that the Red Sox would go on to win the 2004 World Series crown, fulfilling the 86-year-old dream of Red Sox fans everywhere.

# CONTENTS

Seats at Fenway Park

Roger Clemens

Jason Varitek tags out
Mike Napoli.

Carlton Fisk's dramatic
home run

Ted Williams

# RED SOX FANS NEVER FORGET

Michael T. McGreevey owned the Third Base Saloon back in the early 1900s, a place where diehard Boston baseball fans would gather for a shot of passion to inspire daily debates about their beloved team. You know something? Not much has changed.

The Boston Red Sox will always have that effect on New England sports fans. Whether the team is winning or losing in any given year, the sports pages are rife with stories. Meanwhile, radio talk show lines are lit up with debate on all things Red Sox. Summertime means Red Sox, but even in the dead of winter the Red Sox are still on everyone's mind, whether it's awaiting the big trade or a free-agent signing, or counting the days until the manager gets fired.

The heated debates of yesteryear are still heard today at sports bars fashioned after the Third Base Saloon, where fans ponder the same types of issues as they did in the old days. Topics like "Who was better, Pedro or Roger?" or "Was Yaz's Triple Crown season in 1967 a greater feat than Ted Williams's .406 mark in 1941?"

What's amazing is how the ever-growing popularity of the Red Sox has hurdled a number of obstacles through the years. There were fires at Fenway Park in the late '20s and early '30s, which led to major renovations. There were two World Wars, the Korean conflict, and the Vietnam War that took baseball heroes away from the sport and into military service.

There was always something that kept Red Sox fans coming back, whether it was following Ted Williams's every movement in the '40s and '50s or "The Impossible Dream" team kick-starting the fan base for the next 40 years with its improbable quest for the pennant. There were the crushing heartbreaks: the 1946 World Series; Bucky Dent's homer to win the 1978 playoff game; the routine grounder that rolled through Bill Buckner's legs in 1986. Such incidents led to

Ted Williams slides back into first base. The Kansas City first baseman failed to tag him out on this day at Fenway, July 25, 1957. When New Englanders talk about Boston Red Sox greatness, Williams is the first player that comes to their minds.

The Boston Globe's Dan Shaughnessy's coining the phrase "Curse of the Bambino," which referred to owner Harry Frazee's selling Babe Ruth for cash in 1919, a move that many believe brought the Red Sox 86 years of bad karma, broken only by a World Series victory in 2004.

Somehow, probably because of the vast love for this team, fans got over the disappointments and remained loyal. After all, even when there weren't great teams or players, there were colorful characters to watch and enjoy: Jimmy Piersall in the '50s, Ken "Hawk" Harrelson in the '60s, Bill "Spaceman" Lee and "El Tiante" in the '70s, Dennis "Oil Can" Boyd in the '80s, and Mo Vaughn in the '90s.

If you didn't have any of those memories, you always have the ballpark to go to and enjoy. Fenway has undergone facelifts, remodelings, and additions. But since 1912, its basic look and structure have remained intact. It has survived numerous threats from the wrecking ball to become one of the last and most precious links from baseball's past to its present.

But even stronger than the players, the games, the moments, and the ballpark are the personal memories.

Every Red Sox fan can tell you about something that touched them personally over the last 100-plus years of Red Sox baseball. It seems everyone was at Game 6 in 1975 or watched Roger strike out 20 in 1986 or got to see the Splendid Splinter do something extraordinary. Or perhaps it was something as simple as the first time their dad took them to a Red Sox game, complete with details.

Boston Red Sox: Yesterday & Today™ will tell those stories as well as many others, debate the issues, and make you feel as if you're at the Third Base Saloon absorbed in Red Sox talk.

This splendid view of Fenway Park overlooks a game between the Boston Red Sox and Tampa Bay Devil Rays on April 17, 2005. Fenway is one of the oldest and most treasured baseball stadiums in the Major Leagues.

# WELCOME TO FENWAY PARK

LIKE AN OLD HOME passed on to generations of family members, Fenway Park, in spite of its imperfections and age, is a place where Boston fans have lived, loved, cried, laughed, and cheered. Throughout its long history, Fenway has been soothing to the baseball soul. So find a cozy chair, and read the story of a ballpark that is a home, not just a house, to Red Sox Nation.

**Below:** This metal arrow hangs in the bedrooms and basements of thousands of Red Sox fans—all of whom already know how to get to Fenway.

**Bottom of Spread:** Baseball's greatest park opened April 20, 1912. Who opposed the Red Sox? The Yankees, of course (then known as the Highlanders). The good guys won a dramatic extra-inning game that set the stage for nearly a century of baseball's most celebrated rivalry.

## Fenway: New England's Beloved Ballpark

**I**T WAS THE BOTTOM of the third and the count was 2–2 on Red Sox outfielder Ellis Burks, who had stepped out and then dug back into the batter's box while awaiting Chicago White Sox right-hander Jack McDowell's next pitch. The embankment of lights at Fenway Park flickered a little and then a lot. Before McDowell could toss that next pitch on a chilly spring evening of May 13, 1991, at precisely 8:45 P.M., the ballpark went black, eliciting a unified chorus of "ohhhh!" before a hush fell over the 31,023 on hand.

There had been a power failure during a day game in 1981, but this was the first night outage anyone could remember. The entire ballpark was stunned, in panic mode, until a glimmer of auxiliary lighting kicked in around the seating areas, creating sort of a yellow glow. Flashbulbs and cigarette lighters flickered in the darkness from left field to right in one of the most surreal moments Fenway fans had ever experienced. Members of the Fourth Estate (the press) sat in darkness in the press box. Radio and TV outlets were off the air. Patrons couldn't leave their tightly cramped seats.

**Upper Left:** There is never a shortage of trinkets, collectibles, and memorabilia. This key chain has an etched 3-D Fenway Park on one side and the Red Sox logo on the other side.
**Left:** Fenway has been home to many great players but none greater than Ted Williams. In 1940, he was nicknamed "The Kid," and on August 24 of that year, "The Kid" made his major league pitching debut against the Detroit Tigers at Fenway. Of course, he would later become a fixture in left field.

If you were there that night you never forgot it.

The tense situation was alleviated by legendary PA announcer Sherm Feller, who, like a true entertainer, felt that the show must go on. Performing a combination comedy/vaudeville act, Feller joked, "Boston Edison is working on it right now. If they send us a bill, we'll pay it." He then led the crowd through several rounds of "Take Me Out to the Ball Game."

It was literally Fenway's darkest hour. After 59 minutes, power was restored. It was learned later that a manhole cover on Com-

monwealth Avenue had cut off power to the Back Bay.

Ah, Fenway!

That's just one of the countless stories and legends of the ballpark *Boston Globe* owner General Charles H. Taylor built in 1912 in a swampy Boston section known as the Fens. Little did Taylor and his son John know the ballpark would become so famous and later be affectionately called the "lyrical bandbox," the object of affection for poets, baseball purists, authors, and the game's biggest names.

A 1951 view of Fenway Park looking out into right-center field. Ted Williams, Johnny Pesky, and Dom DiMaggio led the charge for the 1951 Red Sox, bringing fans the thrill and excitement that comes with every baseball season in Boston.

# THE FENWAY EXPERIENCE

ONE ARE THE DAYS when children boasted about sneaking into Fenway through undetected openings in the ballpark. While there are no more freebies, with security tight and the ballpark sold out, the Fenway experience now is more about entertainment around the game than it was in yesteryear.

In the early 1900s, some of the diehard Red Sox fans were known as the Royal Rooters, complete with a brass band, scripted cheers, and a lone drumbeat throughout the games. They even had a theme song—"Tessie"—that they played over and over again. It was more like a college football atmosphere than a baseball game.

All you needed were five-cent programs, a scorecard, and a pencil, along with your seat, to enjoy an afternoon in the Fenway sunshine. Although the ballpark was frequently half-empty and TV cameras were absent, the aura was still perfect for Red Sox baseball.

Opening Day at the Fens is like a holiday in New England. Fans old and young anticipate the home opener for weeks and months on end. It's a day when hope springs eternal and memories of yesteryear resurface. The Fenway Faithful were as hopeful as ever when young flamethrower Josh Beckett threw the first pitch of 2006 in the team's home opener against the Toronto Blue Jays.

"As a kid in the early '50s, the focus was on the game and on the players," recalled Red Sox senior adviser Jeremy Kapstein, who grew up in Rhode Island. "As a kid you'd come early and watch Ted Williams take batting practice. He'd walk out of the dugout with two or three bats on his left shoulder, and you'd just watch him hit. There wasn't much going on around the ballpark except for the organ player John Kiley, who would do the National Anthem and play some things during the game. The focus was on the field."

Today mascot "Wally The Green Monster" entertains children and those baseball fans young at heart. The programs are elaborate; team magazines are everywhere; and fans can watch highlights and take Red Sox trivia quizzes on the electronic video monitor.

Popular music blares between innings. "God Bless America" has been sung during the seventh-inning stretch at home Sunday games and on holidays since 9/11. The Red Sox have adopted "Sweet Caroline" by Neil Diamond as a regular song before the bottom of the eighth inning. Fans participate and repeat the line "So good! So good!"

Fans now come to the ballpark far more relaxed in comfortable clothing. In many photos taken of Fenway as late as the 1960s, some men were dressed in suit jackets and ties, going to games directly from work or from church on Sundays.

Another huge change from yesteryear to today: "It was predominantly men and boys," recalled Kapstein. Today, you see many more women in the stands.

"Wally The Green Monster" has become one of the most recognizable mascots in the game. Here's Wally standing tall, carrying the banner for Red Sox Nation.

This is the old front entrance to Fenway Park. Today the front entrance of Fenway is mobbed by fans taking in the food and festivities that come with every Red Sox game day.

# Fenway:
# Through the Decades

FENWAY PARK FEATURES: The Cliff. The Pole. The Triangle. The Wall. The Monster Seats. The Red Seat.

A ballpark that became more lovable the older it got.

A ballpark that has stood the test of time and waited 86 years between championships: from 1918 to 2004.

A ballpark that inspired a passionate group of "Save Fenway" fans in the late 1990s to voice their displeasure over just the thought of Red Sox ownership sketching plans for a new venue.

Designed by Osborn Engineering and built by James McLaughlin Construction for $650,000, Fenway Park opened on April 20, 1912. No one could have predicted then that the quirky little stadium would become a national shrine.

Until then, the Red Sox had played their games at Huntington Avenue Grounds, where prestigious Northeastern University now resides. Huntington was just a ballyard with massive grandstands able to hold 11,500. The first World Series game was played there in 1903 between Boston and Pittsburgh; fans saw Cy Young throw baseball's first 20th-century perfect game. But growing interest in the Red Sox and yearly

Fenway Park has always been one of the premier sports complexes in the country. On April 17, 1956, the Red Sox clobbered the Baltimore Orioles, 8–1, in their home opener.

lease hassles for the Taylors made it inadequate for a fan base starving for a new venue. And Huntington certainly didn't have the lore Fenway would later acquire. There were no "Save Huntington" committees formed anywhere in the city.

Fenway was so named by Taylor after its Fens location. It was originally built to house 27,000 with a single deck. Left field was odd because it featured a 10-foot slope in front of the 37-foot-high left-field wall, designed to keep nonpaying fans out of the park. Left-fielder Duffy Lewis was so good at playing the ball before it went off the ledge that the embankment became known as Duffy's Cliff. It was leveled off in 1934 after a second fire at the ballpark.

Thomas A. Yawkey and his wife, Jean, South Carolina cotton plantation owners, bought the team in 1933 and began rebuilding the ballpark, whose left-field stands had been ravaged by fire on May 8, 1926, and left in disrepair because of insufficient funds. Another fire ruined the ballpark again in 1934, but Yawkey rebuilt it with concrete reinforcement in the seating areas, while a sheet metal structure, which still stands, replaced the 37-foot wooden wall.

In 1936, a 23½-foot net was placed over the left-field wall to protect businesses in the area from having their windows shattered by fly balls. The net remained until seats were built atop the wall in 2004.

*Continued on page 18*

The old wooden seats in the grandstand section of Fenway Park have been bruised and beaten up but have lasted to see some of the great moments in Red Sox history.

SAVE HISTORIC FENWAY PARK

BUILT IN 1912 · A great place for Baseball · Preserve our Tradition · Improve it, don't remove it · www.SaveFenwayPark.com

Thanks to ardent fans who displayed their loyalty to the park with such memorabilia as this Fenway pennant, the Red Sox owners held a press conference on March 23, 2005, to announce that the Red Sox will remain at Fenway Park.

# MEN AT THE MIKE

"**M**ERCY!**"** was the favorite expression of legendary Red Sox broadcaster Ned Martin. Martin was graced with a soothing and mellow voice. Not surprisingly, his poetic calls were heard over the airwaves on both radio and TV from 1961 to 1992, making him the longest tenured and most popular Red Sox broadcaster.

Martin, who died on July 23, 2002, had teamed with two other legendary Red Sox broadcasters, Hall of Famer Curt Gowdy and Ken Coleman, on both radio and TV (1966 to 1972). He called the 1967 World Series on radio and the 1975 World Series for NBC-TV.

Martin also called the pop-up to Rico Petrocelli to clinch the 1967 pennant. And he is known for his call of Roger Clemens's 20-strikeout game in 1986. "Long before there was Morgan's Magic on the field in 1988, there was Martin's Magic on the radio," eulogized *Boston Globe* columnist Bill Griffith.

Meanwhile, Curt Gowdy was the first superstar sports broadcaster. In 1966, he joined NBC, where he called the *Game of the Week* and hosted the popular *American Sportsman* series. Back in Beantown, Gowdy's folksy style resonated with Boston fans. One of the most famous moments in Red Sox history is his call of Ted Williams's final at-bat on September 28, 1960.

After Williams stepped to the plate and the fans at Fenway gave him a standing ovation of

**Above:** Speaking into a microphone on February 27, 1950, is famed sportscaster Curt Gowdy.
**Right:** There was a time when cigarette ads were common on television and in magazines. Here is one featuring Jim Britt, the play-by-play announcer of the Boston Red Sox.

AND WITH THE FANS AT THE HOME GROUNDS OF THE RED SOX AND THE BRAVES CHESTERFIELD IS BY FAR THE LARGEST SELLING CIGARETTE

JIM BRITT — FAMOUS FOR HIS PLAY-BY-PLAY RADIO REPORTS OF THE BOSTON RED SOX AND BRAVES' GAMES

**A** ALWAYS MILDER **B** BETTER TASTING **C** COOLER SMOKING
All the Benefits of Smoking Pleasure

ALWAYS BUY CHESTERFIELD
RIGHT COMBINATION · WORLD'S BEST TOBACCOS · PROPERLY AGED

two minutes, Gowdy described the historic moment: "One out, nobody on, last of the eighth inning. Jack Fisher into his windup, here's the pitch. Williams swings, and there's a long drive to deep right! The ball is going, and it is gone! A home run for Ted Williams in his last time at bat in the major leagues!"

Ken Coleman also had a mellow announcing style in two separate stints with the Red Sox, totaling 20 years. One of his memorable calls came on Carl Yastrzemski's famous tumbling catch at Yankee Stadium on April 14, 1967, to rob Tom Tresh of extra bases and preserve Billy Rohr's no-hit bid in his major league debut. "One of the greatest catches I've ever seen!" exclaimed Coleman on WHDH-TV in Boston.

Former Red Sox second baseman Jerry Remy has become one of baseball's most popular color analysts, known for his superb dissection of the game. Meanwhile, former Red Sox TV announcer Sean McDonough and Don Orsillo have carried on Martin's legacy.

Joe Castiglione began his 25th season as Red Sox radio play-by-play man in 2007, 14 of which featured Jerry Trupiano as analyst/color man. Castiglione called the final out of the clinching game of the 2004 World Series, shouting, "For the first time in 86 years, the Red Sox have won baseball's world championship! Can you believe it?"

Hall of Famer Carl Yastrzemski (right) shares his memories of Red Sox legend Ted Williams with ESPN commentator Peter Gammons (middle) and former Red Sox broadcaster Ned Martin (left) on July 22, 2002.

*Continued from page 15*

By 1946, Yawkey added skybox seats to the single deck ballpark, and a year later lights were turned on at Fenway for the first time. It was in 1947 that advertisements came off The Wall. Because it was painted green, The Wall became known forever as the "Green Monster."

Technology hit Fenway in 1976 when the team erected an electronic scoreboard in center field. But one of the most dramatic changes to the ballpark came in the late 1980s when the Red Sox built glassed-in club seating—which many Red Sox fans say looks out of place—known as the 600 Club at the site of the press box; it was subsequently rebuilt a story higher. In 2005, the glass was removed, the area reconfigured, and it is now called the .406 Club, commemorating Ted Williams's batting average of 1941, one of the best hitting feats in baseball history.

The new construction changed the wind currents, according to Wade Boggs, who was a master of hitting balls to left field, where the wind normally blew out. Boggs, who hit .369 for his career at Fenway, noticed immediately that the structure caused swirling and less predictable winds. MIT later conducted a study that backed Boggs's view. Prior to that ballpark-changing construction, opposing hitters always were enthralled at the thought of playing at Fenway full-time.

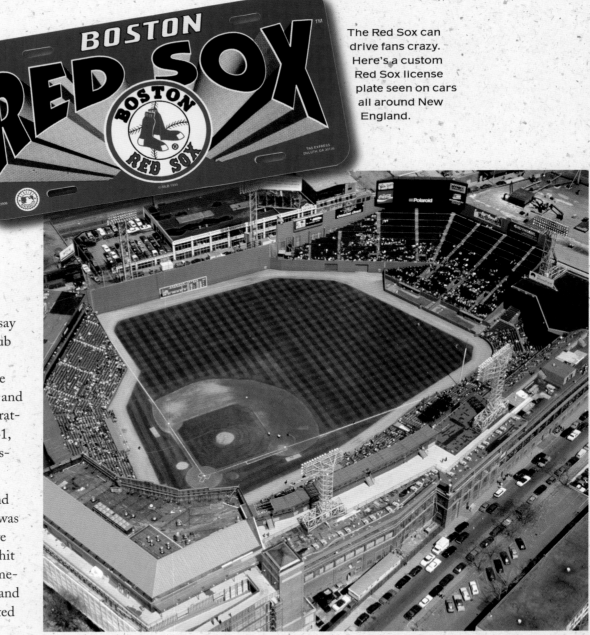

The Red Sox can drive fans crazy. Here's a custom Red Sox license plate seen on cars all around New England.

Fenway Park sits pretty in the middle of Boston next to Kenmore Square. Thousands of Red Sox fans take the Green Line into Fenway every day during the summer to see their hometown heroes. The Red Sox and Fenway Park are important parts of the cultural fabric of Boston.

The sun has set over baseball's most famous wall: the Green Monster. At more than 37 feet high, the Green Monster has witnessed countless Red Sox home run balls soar over it and into the Boston night. It has also robbed many opposing batters of the long ball. Recently added Monster seats have made for one of the most unique viewing experiences in any major league ballpark.

# Fenway:
# A Pitcher's Nightmare

THERE WAS NO GREATER guessing game in its day than the number of dingers Joe DiMaggio would have totaled if he spent his entire career at Fenway with the short porch in left field. Conversely, fans often wondered how many homers Ted Williams might have hit at Yankee Stadium, which favored power-hitting left-hand hitters.

Over the years, considerable affection has come from the mouths of big right-handed sluggers who listed Fenway as their favorite place to hit. Twins slugger Harmon Killebrew once mused, "This ballpark is suited for my swing." The lumberjack-like Frank Howard, at 6′7″, seemed almost as large as the 37-foot wall when he stood at home plate as a clean-up hitter for the Washington Senators in the late 1960s. Hall of Famer Dave Winfield whacked balls so hard off The Wall that he often jested that Fenway reduced the number of his homers.

Despite all the adulation lavished on Fenway by hitters, pitchers and managers often cursed the ballpark. "The sooner they tear down this place the better," Hall of Fame manager Sparky Anderson told a group of reporters in 1991. "This ballpark is laughable. I'd commit suicide if I managed here. It doesn't have mystique. It only gives you a nightmare. Maybe some day they'll take a big bomb and blow it straight up."

*Continued on page 22*

# RED SOX HANGOUTS

**M**cGREEVEY'S Third Base Saloon was Boston's first big sports bar in the early 1900s. It was a place where Red Sox fans, local politicians, and celebrities gathered to talk sports before and after the game. McGreevey himself was famous for settling bar room disputes by slamming his hand on the bar and declaring "Nuf ced!" McGreevey often noted why he named his bar the Third Base Saloon: "You always need to touch third base before heading home."

In Ted Williams's era, the Somerset and Kenmore Hotels were swank postgame spots. There you might catch a glimpse of Williams, as well as other Red Sox players. If you wanted to see stars on other teams, the Kenmore also lodged the visiting teams.

A popular bar near the ballpark was Steve McGrail's Linwood Grill, where players and fans mingled in the '40s, '50s, and '60s. In 1969, when Carl Yastrzemski roamed left field, a local bar called Oliver's opened. Oliver's eventually became the Cask 'n Flagon. It remains the ultimate Red Sox hangout in Boston.

Eccentric pitcher Bill Lee's preferred watering hole was the Elliot Lounge on Commonwealth Avenue. It was also a favorite spot of marathon runners. Nowadays, Red Sox memorabilia covers the wall of the Cask bar as fans bask in the memories of yesteryear. Recently, Game On! has emerged as an ideal spot for hungry and thirsty fans to catch a Red Sox game. And the ever-popular Boston Beer Works provides good food and microbrewed beer.

Dana Van Fleet poses in front of his bar, the Cask 'n Flagon, located at the corner of Brookline Avenue and Lansdowne Street and adjacent to Fenway Park. Cask 'n Flagon boasts of having won several Audience Winner awards for Best Sports Bar.

Around the ballpark prior to game time, fans can be seen on Yawkey Way at RemDawgs, named after former Red Sox second baseman Jerry Remy, who is the popular color commentator on NESN telecasts. At this hangout, fans munch on hot dogs and watch the NESN pregame show. Luis Tiant's Cuban sandwiches are also sold outside the park.

Twins Enterprise began small with pushcarts around Fenway in 1948. By 1967, when the Red Sox went to the World Series, they had established a huge warehouse and one of the largest souvenir stores in America. It is now a popular meeting place before a game.

Red Sox fan hangouts don't end in New England. All across the country, Red Sox bars attract thousands of displaced Red Sox fanatics. Sonny McLean's in Santa Monica, California, offers bus trips for local fans to see the Red Sox play in Anaheim. And can you believe it? Red Sox hangouts are now international with the opening of Fenway Park Public Bar in Kyoto, Japan.

**Above:** The atmosphere outside the park is as spirited as the crowd inside. Here, Red Sox fans in red and blue team colors mob the streets looking for good food, good friends, and good times.
**Right:** You'll find the Red Sox logo everywhere in Boston, even on Coke bottles. Talk about a marketing boom: Here are bottles of 2004 Boston Red Sox-branded Coca-Cola.

*Continued from page 19*

Lefty pitcher David Wells echoed this sentiment. He often spoke of blowing up Fenway, and he even scrawled an expletive inside the large scoreboard area in left field, which precisely captured his feelings for the old yard.

The old-school thought was that Fenway's short porch ate up lefty pitchers. That's why legendary Yankee southpaw Whitey Ford, who made his major league debut at Fenway on July 1, 1950, made only 11 appearances (nine starts) at Fenway Park in his 16-year career. Ford accumulated a disappointing 4–5 record with a 6.44 ERA there. His stats was worse at Fenway than at any other venue.

The Green Monster is a fixture at Fenway Park, and its left-field scoreboard gives Red Sox fans a chance to keep up with how the rest of the league is doing.

# Fenway: Home for Sluggers

ALTHOUGH YANKEE STADIUM is known as The House That Ruth Built, Ruth's illustrious career actually began at Fenway on July 11, 1914, against the Cleveland Indians, two years after Fenway opened. A dominant lefty, Ruth spent four years as a pitcher, logging an amazing 94–46 mound record. He was a fan favorite in Boston before being traded to the Yanks after the 1919 season for $125,000 and a $300,000 mortgage loan on Fenway.

After the Red Sox won the 1918 World Series, Fenway fans wept for almost nine decades in the aftermath of Ruth's departure. Despite the efforts of such great players as Lefty Grove, Joe Cronin, Jimmie Foxx, Bobby Doerr, Ted Williams, Dom DiMaggio, Carl Yastrzemski, Carlton Fisk, Jim Rice, Fred Lynn, Wade Boggs, and Roger Clemens, the Red Sox couldn't capture the World Series crown.

Although Boston fans were thrilled to host the 1946, 1967, 1975, and 1986 World Series at Fenway, they lost each of those series. (Even when the Red Sox won the 1915 and 1916 World Series, they played at Braves Field [Boston], because it had a larger capacity.)

Why not wear a Green Monster pin on your lapel? The Wall was stripped of its billboards in 1937, painted green, and thus nicknamed the Green Monster, a one of a kind.

If the Green Monster had feelings, it would have got goose bumps when Ted Williams stroked a home run in his last at-bat on September 28, 1960, the final day of his career. It might have felt similar feelings during the "Yaz Farewell" on October 2, 1983. On that day, Carl Yastrzemski, Williams's left-field replacement, circled the ballpark, shook hands, and waved his cap. Yaz also said his own farewell to The Wall, where, as a starting left fielder, he had won seven Gold Gloves and perfected taking balls off The Wall to hold hitters to singles.

In 2005, the Red Sox named the left-field pole "Fisk's Pole" to commemorate Carlton Fisk's dramatic arm-waving, 12th-inning, walk-off homer in Game 6 of the 1975 World Series. His game-winning blast soared barely fair down the left-field line to beat the Cincinnati Reds.

*Continued on page 26*

# HOT DOGS, POPCORN, AND SEAFOOD CHOWDER

**R**ED SOX VICE PRESIDENT Dick Bresciani remembers buying hot dogs at Fenway for a quarter in the 1950s, and for countless kids the taste was unforgettable, especially after slopping on some yellow mustard or Gulden's spicy brown. What could be better at the park than eating a dog with a soda and later having a Hood three-flavored ice cream to top it off? Kids from 1 to 92 loved it.

After the '50s, you probably sipped on a Gansett (Narragansett beer) and munched on popcorn or peanuts. Later in the game, you might have a slice of pizza or a pretzel—a menu that was pretty much the standard through the '60s, '70s, and part of the '80s.

Then the Red Sox marketing department began to create deals with other food venues. Harry M. Stevens Co. was the longtime concessionaire at Fenway. But after Aramark took over the concessions in the 1990s, fancy stuff like Legal Seafood clam chowder and Kowloon Chinese food began to spring up, and now an extensive selection of bottled

Kolder/ MLBP 2006

**Left:** Food and drinks are in no short supply in and around Fenway Park. Beers of the World is a popular spot on Yawkey Way for Red Sox fans to indulge in a wide variety of beers from around the globe.
**Far Left:** You'll see many fans with Koozie MLB bottle holders at the ballpark. The holders not only keep drinks cold but also display the Red Sox logo.

domestic and imported beers are offered. Meanwhile, other food, such as steak tips, hamburgers, pizza, and salads, have appeared around the ballyard. There's even a picnic-style concession area in right field with all the modern food selections.

There have always been sausage vendors outside the ballpark. Today, their numbers are extensive. Peanuts, pistachios, cashews—all kinds of nuts—are available from small vendors and concessionaires right outside Fenway's gates. They also serve everything from pizza slices to steak and cheese subma-rines to hamburgers with all the fixings.

Dogs are no longer a quarter, and nothing is 50 cents or a dollar anymore. Concession prices are very high—$5 to $7 for a beer, $4.25 for a bottle of water, and $5 for a Papa Gino's individual pizza.

What else has changed? For ice cream, how about a Cool Dog? It's basically ice cream and cake that looks like a hot dog on a bun.

On April 11, 2006, Red Sox fans enjoyed snacks at tables outside Fenway before their team's home opener. Championship banners were proudly displayed above them.

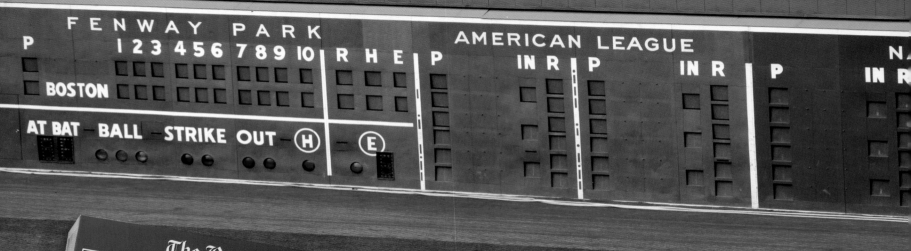

The Boston Globe

RAINBOWS OVER FENWAY PARK

WHITE MOUNTAIN PUZZLES

550 PIECE PUZZLE

July 7, 2000 Boston: A double rainbow lingered over Fenway Park during a Friday night game.

**Top of Page:**
The Red Sox score-
board below the Green Monster is
among the few manual scoreboards in major
league baseball. Green and red lights are
used to signal balls, strikes, and outs. It's a
great way to keep up to date on the Red Sox
game at hand, as well as keep tabs on the
Yankees.
**Above:** There's something for everyone
in Red Sox Nation, even puzzle lovers.
*Rainbows Over Fenway Park* is one of many
jigsaw puzzles produced by White Mountain
Puzzles.

*Continued from page 23*

One more thing about Fenway's left field: It remains the only outfield in major league baseball where a ground rule triple can be had if you hit the ladder attached to the manual scoreboard in left center.

Right field at Fenway is certainly low profile compared to left. Nonetheless, there are memorable aspects of the opposite side of Fenway. On June 9, 1946, 56-year-old Joe Boucher was sitting in Section 42, Row 37, Seat 21—502 feet from home plate—when Ted Williams's prodigious blast off Detroit's Fred Hutchinson knocked the straw hat off his head. Boucher, asked whether he had tried to secure the souvenir, said, "After it hit my head, I was no longer interested."

Left-hand sluggers, such as Carl Yastrzemski, Mo Vaughn, and David Ortiz, all hit long homers to right but never quite so far as Williams's immortal blast. "They keep moving that seat farther away," lamented Ortiz.

No hitter has ever hit one over the right-field roof at Fenway. There's also the tricky right-field railing, which has swallowed up many a right fielder over the years. Dwight Evans—perhaps Boston's best defensive right fielder ever—had mastered the railing close to Pesky's Pole and the curvatures in right center mastered. Outfielder Wily Mo Pena, playing for the Cincinnati Reds in 2005, ran toward the railing on a Manny Ramirez fly ball and got so squeamish that he clumsily stuck his mitt out and watched the ball bounce off the heel of his glove and into the right-field seats for a home run.

Beloved local hero Tony Conigliaro was known for leaping into the bullpen to make incredible catches. Tom Brunansky secured the final out to clinch the 1990 AL East title with a catch in the corner, which was so obscured by cheering and arm-waving fans that few people actually saw it.

Of course, right field is home to Pesky's Pole, named after Red Sox shortstop Johnny Pesky, who has six career homers at Fenway Park to his credit (17 overall). After Pesky homered to win a game in 1948, starting pitcher Mel Parnell dubbed the pole "Pesky's Pole." The name stuck.

Tom Yawkey had bullpens built in right field in 1940, which brought the fences in 23 feet to accommodate young slugger Ted Williams, who hit so many homers there that the pen became known as "Williamsburg."

The right-field facade is also home to Boston's retired numbers: 1, 4, 8, 9, and 27 in honor of Hall of Fame second baseman Bobby Doerr, former Red Sox shortstop and AL president Joe Cronin, Yastrzemski, Williams, and Fisk, respectively.

The Triangle (center field) was and is one of the most unique spots in baseball. Hit it there, and it's a triple. It's also a place where such speedy outfielders as Tris Speaker, Dom DiMaggio, Jimmy Piersall, Fred Lynn, Ellis Burks, and Johnny Damon made some of their finest catches.

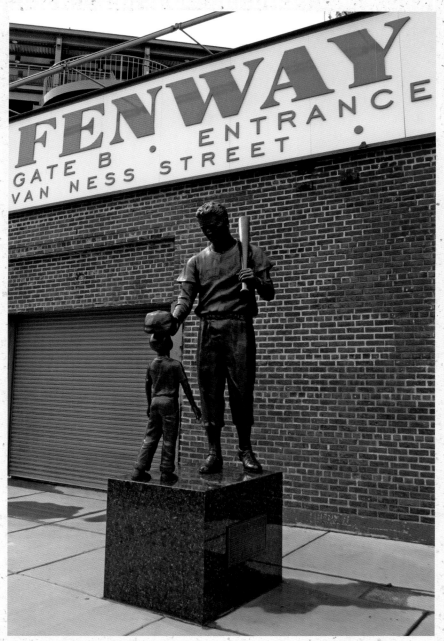

Ted Williams was respected by his peers, acclaimed by analysts, and idolized by kids. A statue of Ted Williams placing a cap on a young fan's head can be seen outside of Gate B at Fenway Park.

# COOL STUFF
## (MEMORABILIA THEN AND NOW)

ONE OF THE GREAT people-watching exercises while catching a game at Fenway is seeing the mountains of merchandise that proud members of Red Sox Nation display. Some days it seems as if everybody in the yard is sporting their favorite player's jersey.

Red Sox caps can be found covering the heads of not only Red Sox diehards but Bostonians of all kinds. You can see Red Sox lovers sport the hometown team's merchan-

dise everywhere in Boston, especially when the Red Sox are playing the hated Yankees. In fact, Boston fans also love to wear anti-Yankee attire.

The scene at the park is drastically different than the days when Babe Ruth and Tris Speaker roamed the outfield. In the old days, Red Sox fans could be found in top

**Above:** A baseball autographed by Red Sox captain Jason Varitek is just one of the countless items fans can purchase at souvenir shops around Fenway.

**Left:** The Souvenir Shop on Yawkey Way has any piece of memorabilia a true Red Sox fan desires—from apparel to autographs and everything in between, The Souvenir Shop and vendors like it are packed on game day.

hats, suits, and gowns. Such was that era in which fans dressed to the nines to catch a game at Fenway.

In 1967, people collected loaves of "Yaz Bread" that some fans still have frozen in their basement freezers. There's also *The Impossible Dream*, an album on which former Red Sox voice Ken Coleman and local broadcaster Don Gillis take you through the incredible 1967 season. Tony Conigliaro cut a couple of 45s, one called "Playing the Field." There are still shots of Ted Williams's Sears ads.

Today, it's all about team colors and representing the good guys. One of the new fashion fads at Fenway is pink hats and jerseys for female fans. Never before has the team enjoyed such a strong female fan base, thanks in large part to the cool memorabilia available to all fans.

After the 2004 World Series championship, memorabilia collecting has been at an all-time high as many fans have invested in anything displaying the 2004 Red Sox. One of the coolest items Red Sox fans hang on their walls are copies of *The Boston Globe*'s front page after the Red Sox swept the Cardinals to win it all in 2004.

From key chains to banners, signed bats and balls to framed portraits, there is sure to be something different in every Red Sox fan's living room. Moreover, there is merchandise available to fit any season. If it's summertime, fans can break out their Boston Red Sox logo beach towels. If the weather calls for rain,

they can buy a Fenway park umbrella to keep them dry. Mugs, night lights, calendars, pins, magnets, plaques, DVDs, books, jewelry… you name it, and Red Sox Nation is proudly showing it off.

**Above:** Pink Red Sox caps can be found throughout Fenway Park. The Henry-Luccino-Werner administration has done an outstanding job of marketing the club to its female fans.
**Right:** The 2004 World Series not only brought years of Boston heartache to an end but also started a merchandise explosion the likes of which New Englanders had never seen. The 2004 Red Sox became the most popular brand in town. One such item is this 2004 World Series Champions cap.

On April 11, 2006, the Red Sox, led by David Ortiz, set out for another season filled with drama, angst, and triumph that can be seen only in Boston.

## Fenway:
## Remember Those Other Teams?

**D**ESPITE THE MEMORABLE baseball played at Fenway Park over the years, we can't forget that the ballpark also served as a home to professional football. After Yawkey revitalized the ballpark in 1933, the Boston Redskins played their home games there from 1933 to 1936. Attendance, however, was so poor that owner George Preston Marshall decided to play the NFL Championship game at New York's Polo Grounds rather than at Fenway. The Redskins lost 21–6 to the Green Bay Packers and moved to Washington in 1937.

In 1944, the Boston Yanks played at Fenway during World War II. They also couldn't muster much interest and folded in 1948. New England fans, however, came back in 1963 when the Boston Patriots, a top American Football League team at the time, moved to Fenway and drew big crowds on frigid late fall and winter days. About 5,000 temporary seats were constructed to house fans backed against the Green Monster, with the goal lines ranging from the third base line to right field.

There was even professional soccer. Yes, let us not forget the Boston Beacons, who turned the diamond into a soccer field in 1968. Indeed, the ballpark keeps reinventing itself with wider concourses, more concessions, and rooftop seats in right field.

While the lights have gone out at Tiger Stadium, old Comiskey Park, and old Yankee Stadium, the lights remain on at Fenway Park—with the electric bill paid in full for years to come for Boston's cherished Red Sox.

**Top:** Red Sox fans show support for their hometown team by wearing everything from jerseys and hats to foam fingers and pins. This red Fenway Park pin, "Established April 20, 1912," shows that the team's history is an integral part of Red Sox Nation.
**Above:** Fenway Park is "America's Most Beloved Ballpark" and the home of the 2004 and 2007 World Series champions. Historic Fenway has hosted some of the greatest moments in baseball history, and the atmosphere is second to none.

# TEN REASONS TO LOVE THE RED SOX

THEY WERE TEN TEAMS that stuck in your heart and mind, sparking the passion of youth or acting as a simple remembrance of a blissful time. They were sentimental journeys of the Boston baseball soul.

"BABE" RUTH
P.—Boston Red Sox
147

The 1918 Red Sox captured the franchise's last championship before an 86-year drought. Babe Ruth, seen in his Red Sox uniform in the two pictures to the right, was sold to the New York Yankees for $100,000 after the 1919 season during a period in which owner Harry Frazee sold off many top Red Sox players. Ruth would go on to become an American icon, while the Red Sox struggled for decades to return to prominence. That is, until 2004.

**Above:** Johnny Damon triples in the sixth inning of Game 4 of the 2004 World Series against the St. Louis Cardinals. The long-haired former center fielder hit a solo home run in the first inning of Game 4, setting the tone for what would be the clinching game in a World Series sweep.

**Top Right:** Bobby Doerr and his autograph are featured on this postcard though his last name is misspelled in white. Doerr played his entire 14-year career with the Boston Red Sox at second base from the late '30s to the early '50s.

**Right:** "Impossible Dreamer" Jim Lonborg was the ace of the 1967 Red Sox rotation. Lonborg posted a 3.16 ERA en route to the Cy Young Award. The following year, not surprisingly, Lonborg's button was very popular.

# 1903

THE BOSTON AMERICANS (who became the Red Sox) were the oldest franchise in the American League in 1903. They had their own fan club—the Royal Rooters—complete with a brass band and a team song, "Tessie," which was played over and over again at Huntington Avenue Grounds.

The 1903 squad featured three 20-plus game winners—the immortal Cy Young, Long Tom Hughes, and Bill Dineen. They stormed into first place on June 23 behind Buck Freeman (104 RBI) and Patsy Dougherty (.331 average). By September 2, they had opened up a double-digit lead, eventually finishing the regular season 14 1/2 games up to win the American League pennant.

That spring on May 7, the Americans had defeated the New York Highlanders (who became the Yankees) 6–2, in the first game of what became the Red Sox-Yankees rivalry. The three-game series was action-packed and included bad blood. New York outfielder Dave Fultz ran over Americans pitcher George Winter on a cover play at first base, igniting the feud that would supply years of Red Sox-Yankees drama.

But the climax of the 1903 season was Boston's victory in the first World Series. The Americans beat the Pittsburgh Pirates of the National League, five games to three.

**Above:** The 1903 Boston team (known then as the Boston Americans) won the first ever Major League Baseball World Series by defeating the Pittsburgh Pirates five games to three. Cy Young posted a 28–9 record in 1903 with a 2.08 ERA. The Americans went on to become the dominant team of the next two decades. **Left:** Most sports collectors would welcome this fascinating Cy Young tobacco tin, which includes his autograph, into their baseball memorabilia.

# 1915

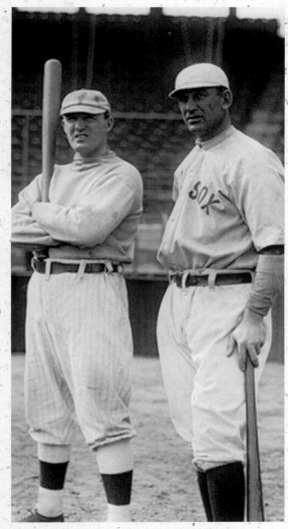

Manager Jake Stahl (right) led the Red Sox to the 1912 World Series championship. The team's platoon catcher was Bill Carrigan (left), who became the manager the following year. His Red Sox teams won the World Series in 1915 and 1916.

Legendary Philadelphia A's manager Connie Mack predicted on February 28, 1915, to *The Washington Post*, "I believe the Boston Red Sox have an edge, but my club will surely have to be reckoned with."

Mr. Mack was half right. Red Sox manager Bill Carrigan's nine went 101–50, winning the AL pennant in a nip-and-tuck battle with the White Sox and Tigers. Smoky Joe Wood posted a 1.49 ERA (though he suffered from a sore arm most of the season), and Rube Foster (19–8), Babe Ruth (18–8), and Dutch Leonard (15–7) led a formidable staff. Center fielder/leadoff hitter Tris Speaker hit .322.

One of the greatest games in Red Sox history to that point was played on September 18. Red Sox pitcher Ernie Shore went 12 innings to defeat Ty Cobb's Tigers in a six-hit shutout before 37,528 at Fenway to take a three-game lead with 15 games left.

The Red Sox went on to win their third world championship, defeating the Philadelphia Phillies four games to one.

Smoky Joe Wood was one of the premier pitchers of his era, and though 1915 was his last year with the Red Sox before ending his career with the Cleveland Indians, he won 15 games for them that year.

# UNIFORM DESIGNS COME AND GO

Tʜᴇ Bᴏꜱᴛᴏɴ Rᴇᴅ Sᴏx players never had to feel the embarrassment of wearing those short pants that legendary Chicago White Sox owner Bill Veeck introduced to the league in the 1970s. Or, for that matter, those ugly, bright, eye-popping jerseys the Houston Astros used for so many years.

The style of the Red Sox uniforms has been rather conservative and traditional through the years. In fact, they were one of the last teams to switch from a laced-front jersey to the button-down style every team wore by 1910. The Red Sox haven't made many changes since then.

Their blue caps with a red "B" first appeared in 1933, replacing the white caps with red trim that they had worn since 1921. They also introduced a uniform with pin-stripes in 1921, which was worn until 1931.

Uniform numbers didn't come until after the Indians and Yankees started the trend in 1929. Forty-three years later, the Red Sox switched to tight-fitting, polyester, pull-over, V-neck jerseys, which didn't go over with the players. Nevertheless, the Red Sox kept those jerseys through the 1978 season. Then they reverted to a button-down with red piping

1923 BASE BALL UNIFORM SAMPLES

MANUFACTURED BY
CHARLES C. CARR CO.
INDIANAPOLIS

SOLD BY

May & Malone, Inc.
29 E. Madison St.
Chicago, Ill.

**Above:** Red Sox uniform styles have changed minimally through the years. Here, Harry Hooper, Tris Speaker, and Duffy Lewis (from left to right) sport baggy jerseys from the 1910s.

**Left:** By the time Cy Young posed for this 1923 baseball uniform catalog, he had long retired from the game and had already become a living legend.

and blue lettering on their white home "RED SOX" jerseys. They had a similar gray style for road games with "BOS-TON" across the front. They also switched to all red stirrups, eliminating the blue stripes.

By 1990, the road uniforms had changed from blue to red lettering on "BOSTON." By 1995, the blue stripes had returned on the socks, and by 2004, there was no sign of socks except on players who chose to show them (pitcher Mike Timlin for example).

Ted Williams was one of the first players to use the "low-roll" style of pants, which covered part of the socks. By the late 1990s, Manny Ramirez had taken it to the extreme; his pant legs were tied onto his cleats.

"All I ever cared about was that the uniform said 'Boston' or 'Red Sox' across the front of it," said Carl Yastrzemski.

# 1918

**W**ORLD WAR I robbed baseball of many star players in 1918, but the Red Sox had Babe Ruth. It was the year when Ruth showcased his legendary ability as a pitcher *and* a slugger. While he jumped the team for a few days in July for Chester Shipyards in Pennsylvania, he returned to lead Boston to a World Series.

Ruth balked at pitching and wanted to be a full-time hitter, but he went 13–7 as a pitcher and hit .300 with 11 homers in 95 games. Because of the shortage of players, many teams, including the Red Sox, used players in multiple roles. Ruth hit ninth when he pitched and also played the outfield and first base.

Tragically, world events overshadowed the last Boston Red Sox championship season before an 86-year drought. This team easily won the American League pennant with a 75–51 record in a season shortened by the war, and it prevailed over the Chicago Cubs in the World Series for their fifth championship title.

Babe Ruth, Ernie Shore, Rube Foster, and Del Gainer (from left to right) look on from the dugout. These four were part of the core Red Sox teams that won back-to-back World Series titles in 1915 and 1916.

# 1946

**T**ED WILLIAMS RETURNED from three years of World War II military duty to post a .342 average with 38 homers and 123 RBI. Indeed, he was the centerpiece of an offensive machine that ripped through the American League. The Red Sox, who won the AL title by 12 games, were in first place on April 28 and never lost their lead. They were the last Red Sox team to win more than 100 games (104).

Williams, Bobby Doerr, Dom DiMaggio, Johnny Pesky, and Rudy York, along with pitcher Tex Hughson, propelled Boston to the World Series against the St. Louis Cardinals. It was a hard-fought series, but they lost in seven games.

Amazingly, Williams was the subject of trade rumors. New Englanders were in an uproar. How could the organization even consider such a preposterous idea? Red Sox owner Thomas Yawkey tried to assure the public by telling the Boston newspapers at the end of the season, "We will definitely not trade Ted Williams."

**Above:** Ted Williams, Bobby Doerr, Dom DiMaggio, and Johnny Pesky were close friends, which David Halberstam described in his book *The Teammates*.
**Middle:** What Red Sox fan would not want a baseball autographed by Ted Williams? Without a doubt, Williams epitomizes Red Sox greatness.
**Right:** At times, it was rumored that the Red Sox would swap Ted Williams to the Yankees for Joe DiMaggio—one immortal baseball player for another. Here Williams (left) and DiMaggio celebrate the American League All-Stars' victory over the National League All-Stars on July 8, 1941.

# OWNERS THEN AND NOW

**A**NY FRANCHISE WITH an enduring legacy of success has to be led by dedicated owners who have the best interests of the team in mind. Red Sox Nation had Tom Yawkey then and John Henry now.

The most reviled Red Sox owner in Red Sox history is Harry Frazee, who sold Babe Ruth to the rival Yankees on December 26, 1919, allegedly in order to finance his Broadway play, *No, No, Nanette*. Frazee had rid the club of other popular stars in prior years, and he continued to anger fans by selling Red Sox stars after he gave birth to the "Curse of the Bambino." The result was that the Red Sox became a second-division team in the 1920s and 1930s. Red Sox fortunes changed, however, when Yawkey bought the team in 1933.

Yawkey brought in such baseball greats as Lefty Grove, Joe Cronin, Jimmie Foxx, and, in 1939, Ted Williams. Once again, the Red Sox became a competitive team. Tom Yawkey, until his death in 1976, and his wife, Jean, thereafter, obtained and recruited some of the greatest players in Red Sox history. Other superstars were Carl Yastrzemski, Carlton Fisk, Jim Rice, Mo Vaughn, and Roger Clemens. Spanning several decades, many Red Sox legends have played for the Yawkey administration.

**Left:** In 1919 Red Sox owner Harry Frazee sold George Herman Ruth to the New York Yankees for $100,000. This single act would become the centerpiece for the famed "Curse of the Bambino" saga that would define Red Sox baseball for decades to come.
**Below:** Former Red Sox owner Tom Yawkey sits next to his wife, Jean, in 1936. Yawkey purchased the club in 1933 and turned it back into one of the top franchises in the sport, presiding over three American League championship teams.

Yawkey brought an aggressive style to team ownership that was rare for his era. Unafraid to spend big money for big players, he also rebuilt Fenway twice after the stadium was ravaged by fire. Yawkey was ultracompetitive, which had a trickle-down effect through the organization to the coaches, players, and fans.

In addition, the Yawkeys felt the team had an obligation to give to charity and be of service to the community. In the 1950s, they accepted the Jimmy Fund as the primary charitable partner to the Red Sox organization, with the help of the legendary Ted Williams. Though criticized for being the last owner to hire an African-American player (Pumpsie Green in 1959), Tom Yawkey was inducted into the Baseball Hall of Fame in 1980.

After Jean Yawkey's death in 1992, control of the team passed to the Yawkey Trust, led by John Harrington. After 70 years in the hands of the Yawkey administration, the team was sold to John Henry in 2002. Like Yawkey back in the 1930s, John Henry has made fan-friendly modifications to Fenway Park. The Henry group added seats atop the famed Green Monster in Fenway's left field, making for one of the most unique viewing experiences in all of American sports.

On the baseball side, Henry hired general manager Theo Epstein, then only 28 years old. The one thing Henry, a hedge-fund mogul, accomplished in a short time that the Yawkeys never did? A World Championship.

One caveat, however: Several members of the 2004 championship team came from the Yawkey era.

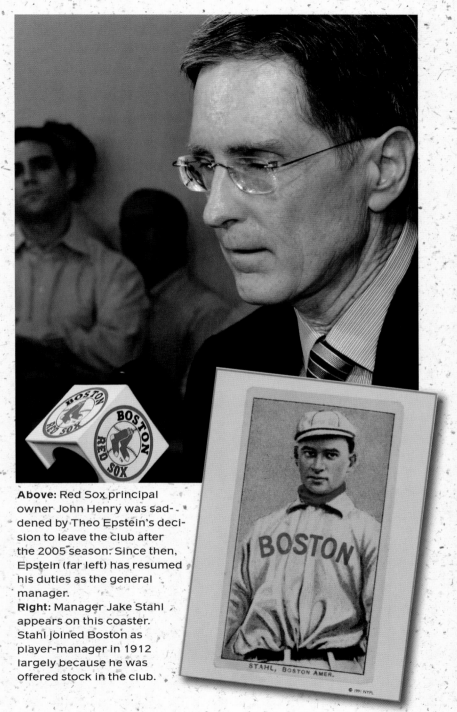

**Above:** Red Sox principal owner John Henry was saddened by Theo Epstein's decision to leave the club after the 2005 season. Since then, Epstein (far left) has resumed his duties as the general manager.
**Right:** Manager Jake Stahl appears on this coaster. Stahl joined Boston as player-manager in 1912 largely because he was offered stock in the club.

STAHL, BOSTON AMER.

# 1967

**S**HORTSTOP RICO PETROCELLI secured the final out on a Rich Rollins pop-up as the Red Sox beat the Twins 5–3 at Fenway on the final day of the season, clinching a tie for the American League pennant. "It seemed that pop-up stayed up there for an eternity," recalled Petrocelli. "I don't think we ever realized what we had accomplished until many years later."

The team then turned the TV on in the clubhouse to watch the end of Detroit's second game of a doubleheader against the California Angels. When the Tigers lost, the Red Sox, known as the "Cardiac Kids," had realized their "Impossible Dream."

Petrocelli was right. It was the only time in Red Sox history when nobody dwelled on the World Series (which they lost to the St. Louis Cardinals in seven games). It was the regular season that mattered. Reggie Smith, George Scott, Joe Foy, Mike Andrews, Tony Conigliaro, Jim Lonborg, Petrocelli, and, of course, Carl "Yaz" Yastrzemski had vaulted the team from ninth place in 1966 to first under the direction of rookie manager Dick Williams.

That memorable year, Yaz became the last major-leaguer to win baseball's coveted Triple Crown.

**Below:** The 1967 Red Sox season is appropriately referred to as the "Impossible Dream." Hall of Famer Carl Yastrzemski led the old-town team to the American League pennant, after the Red Sox had struggled for much of the decade. It was a true roller-coaster season that no fan lucky enough to have witnessed it will ever forget.

**Above:** The 1967 Red Sox season was so special that a tribute album entitled *The Impossible Dream* was released. The album was narrated by former Red Sox announcer Ken Coleman.

# 1975

LET US NOT FORGET the gyrations of big-game savant *El Tiante*, the enthusiasm of "Gold Dust Twins" Fred Lynn and Jim Rice, the bizarre fun of Bill Lee, and Pudge's Game 6 homer and wave in 1975. Colorful Sox outfielder Bernie Carbo said several years after the 1975 season, "It was the best time of our lives."

Opening Day (April 8) at Fenway marked the American League debut of Henry Aaron for the Milwaukee Brewers and a return to baseball for beloved No. 25 Tony Conigliaro. Luis Tiant won the game 5–2, and the Red Sox went on to win 95 games.

The Red Sox won six straight games in early May, and they were buoyed by Tiant, who bested Nolan Ryan of the Angels 6–1 on May 23. On June 18, rookie Fred Lynn, the first player to win both Rookie of the Year and MVP honors in the same season, hit three homers and drove in ten against the Tigers.

The Red Sox won ten straight before and after the All-Star break and held comfortable leads. After Jim Rice's left hand was broken by a Vern Ruhle pitch on September 21, the Red Sox barely held on to win the pennant.

The Red Sox swept the Oakland A's, who had won the three previous World Series, in the AL playoffs. They subsequently played in arguably the greatest World Series ever, facing the Cincinnati Reds. The "Big Red Machine" edged them by scoring the winning run in the ninth inning of the seventh game.

**Above:** The charismatic Luis Tiant owned the Fenway Park mound through much of the 1970s. *El Tiante*, as he was affectionately called by the Fenway faithful, won 20 games three times and helped lead the club to the 1975 World Series.
**Right:** Like Hall of Famers Ted Williams and Carl Yastrzemski, Jim Rice played his entire career for the Boston Red Sox as a power-hitting left fielder.

# INTIMIDATING RED SOX LINEUPS

**H**ERE ARE TWO All-Star lineups, one from the start of the live ball era up through 1986 vs. an All-Star lineup after 1986. Who'd win?

## Through 1986

1B—Jimmie Foxx: The 1938 MVP tallied an amazing .349 with 50 homers and 175 RBI.

2B—Bobby Doerr: In 1950, Doerr hit 27 homers and knocked in 120 runs with a .294 batting average.

SS—Joe Cronin: As a 33-year-old player-manager in 1940, Cronin belted 24 homers and drove in 111 runs.

3B—Frank Malzone: In 1957, Malzone smacked .292 with 15 homers and 103 RBI.

C—Carlton Fisk: In 1977, Fisk totaled .315 with 26 homers and 102 RBI for the Red Sox.

LF—Carl Yastrzemski: In 1967, Yaz won the Triple Crown with a .326 BA, 44 homers, and 121 RBI.

CF—Dom DiMaggio: He stroked .328 with seven homers and 70 RBI in 1950.

RF—Dwight Evans: In 1982, he slugged 32 homers, plated 98 runs, and ripped .292.

DH—Ted Williams: No DH in his era, but we're pretending Williams would be it. In 1941, he became the last man to hit over .400 (.406) while amassing 37 homers and 120 RBI.

SP—Roger Clemens: He was 24–4 and the Cy Young and MVP winner in 1986.

**Top:** With the sweetest swing in baseball history, Williams was both a hitter and a slugger. There were no holes in his swing, and it was virtually impossible to fool Williams with any type of pitch.
**Above Right:** In the '60s, Yaz graced the covers of many sports magazines, such as this 1968 issue of *Baseball* quarterly.
**Left:** A young "Rocket" is shown set for blastoff early in his career. Roger Clemens, one of the sport's most decorated pitchers, set the record for most strikeouts in a single game with 20 on April 29, 1986. En route to three Cy Young Awards and a league MVP crown, Clemens tied Cy Young's franchise record of 192 career wins.

# Post-1986

**1B—Mo Vaughn:** He won the MVP in 1995 but had an even better year in 1996 with a .326 BA, 44 homers, and 143 RBI.

**2B—Todd Walker:** In 2003, his only season in Boston, he stroked .283 with 13 homers and 85 RBI.

**SS—Nomar Garciaparra:** He won the batting title with a .372 average in 2000, while belting 21 homers and driving in 96.

**3B—Wade Boggs:** Boggs clobbered 24 homers, knocked in 89 runs, and ripped .363 in 1987.

**C—Jason Varitek:** In 2003, he smacked .273 with 25 homers and 85 RBI.

**LF—Manny Ramirez:** In 2002, he hit .349, tallied 33 homers and 107 RBI, and posted a .450 on-base average and a .647 slugging percentage.

**CF—Johnny Damon:** In 2004, this leadoff hitter rapped .304 with 20 homers, 94 RBI, 19 stolen bases, and a .380 on-base percentage.

**RF—Trot Nixon:** Nixon stroked .306 with 28 homers and 87 RBI in 2003.

**DH—David Ortiz:** In 2006, Ortiz hit .287 with a team-record 54 homers, 137 RBI, and 119 walks.

**SP—Pedro Martinez:** In 1999, pitching Triple Crown winner Martinez went 23–4 with 313 strikeouts and a 2.07 ERA in 213$\frac{1}{3}$ innings.

**Above:** The 2003 ALCS renewed the postseason rivalry between the Red Sox and Yankees and heightened it to levels never before seen. Here, Manny Ramirez takes Mike Mussina deep in Game 1.
**Right:** Grady Little's decision to leave a tired Pedro Martinez in the game for the eighth inning went down in history as one of the most controversial non-calls ever made by a Red Sox manager. The Red Sox would go on to lose the game and the series to their blood rivals, the Yankees.

# 1978

IF EVER A TEAM was perfectly suited for Fenway Park, it was the 1978 squad. The Red Sox were 57–26 at the All-Star break, an incredible 34–6 at Fenway. They had a nine-game lead over Milwaukee at the break, 14½ over the Yankees. "By far the most talented team I ever played on," said former Sox second baseman Jerry Remy.

Perhaps all that's remembered, however, is how the Red Sox squandered that huge lead to the Yanks. The collapse began in the early September Boston Massacre against the Yanks at Fenway in which the Red Sox were outscored 42–9. It culminated with Yankee Bucky Dent smashing a three-run homer to win the infamous playoff game for the AL Eastern Division championship.

Jim Rice, who hit .361 at Fenway with 28 of his 46 home runs, led a talented team of seven All-Stars, including Fred Lynn, Carl Yastrzemski, Carlton Fisk, Jerry Remy, Rick Burleson, and Dwight Evans. In addition, Dennis Eckersley won 20, Mike Torrez earned 16 wins, and Bob Stanley went 15–2 in relief. But in the end, these achievements were to no avail.

Dwight "Dewey" Evans won eight Gold Glove Awards while patrolling one of the trickiest right fields in all of baseball. He also boasted a powerful, accurate throwing arm.

The "Eck" had two stints with the Red Sox, one as a starting pitcher early in his career in which he was a 20-game winner in Boston's tragic 1978 season. Eckersley, a Hall of Famer after an incredible career as a closer in Oakland, also spent the final season of his career (1998) with the Red Sox.

# 1986

O N A CHILLY April 29 night, 24-year-old Roger Clemens struck out 20 Seattle Mariners at Fenway Park before 13,414 fans in one of the most dominating displays of pitching ever seen. "I've never seen a pitcher hit a spot in the mitt any more consistently than Roger," said his catcher, Rich Gedman. "And with velocity and movement and a look in his eyes that he could strike you out at any time."

Clemens's Cy Young/MVP season carried the 1986 Red Sox to the playoffs in which they survived Game 5 of the American League Championship Series. Dave Henderson staved off elimination by the California Angels with a ninth-inning two-run homer with two outs off closer Donnie Moore. After the Angels tied it, Henderson struck with a sacrifice fly in the 11th to win it. The Red Sox won the next two games in Boston to face the Mets in the World Series.

One of the most talked-about errors in Red Sox history occurred when a slow roller passed under the mitt of first baseman Bill Buckner in the bottom of the tenth inning at Shea Stadium. The Mets scored the winning run on that play to take Game 6 of the World Series, and two days later they became world champions. Although some have cast Buckner as the villain, it was really the collapse of the bullpen that cost the Red Sox the series.

**MASSACHUSETTS MAY84**
**No. 615194**
**CLEMENS 21**

**Above:** Roger Clemens left a lasting impact on Red Sox Nation. The "Clemens 21" license plate is no doubt a collector's item for fans of "The Rocket."
**Right:** Roger Clemens has won seven Cy Young Awards, more than any pitcher in MLB history. He has done it with four different teams in three different decades. Despite his success elsewhere, the Rocket's stint with the Red Sox was what made him a legend.

# FUN FACTS

• The initials of long-time Red Sox owners Tom and Jean Yawkey are inscribed in the manual scoreboard in left field ... in Morse Code.

• "The Star-Spangled Banner" was played during the seventh-inning stretch of the first game of the 1918 World Series between the Red Sox and Cubs. It was to honor those American soldiers who were fighting in Europe at the time. It soon became a baseball tradition.

• Before legendary Fenway groundskeeper Joe Mooney worked for the Red Sox, he took care of D.C. (which became RFK) Stadium in Washington when Vince Lombardi was the coach of the Redskins and Ted Williams managed the Senators.

• Famous oddsmaker Jimmy "The Greek" Snyder had the Red Sox as 100–1 underdogs to win the American League pennant prior to the start of the 1967 season.

• In Game 2 of the 1916 World Series, Babe Ruth pitched a 14-inning, complete-game, 2–1 win over the Brooklyn Dodgers. He is the only World Series starting pitcher not to bat in the ninth position.

The 1918 World Series would be Boston's fifth and final world championship victory of the century. Boston defeated the Chicago Cubs four games to two.

• Through the 2006 season, 206 positional players and 98 pitchers had played for both the Red Sox and the New York Yankees.

• Shortstop John Valentin pulled off the last unassisted Red Sox triple play on July 8, 1994, in the sixth inning vs. Seattle at Fenway Park. Valentin caught a line drive off the bat of Marc Newfield, touched second to retire Mike Blowers, and tagged Kevin Mitchell hung up between first and second to complete the triple play.

• Smoky Joe Wood holds the Red Sox record for most consecutive games won—16—in 1912.

• Jon Lester pitched the last no-hitter by a Red Sox pitcher, a 17–0 win over Kansas City on May 19, 2008. There have been 19 official no-hitters pitched in Red Sox history. Only one was a perfect game; Cy Young pitched it on May 5, 1904, a 3–0 win over Philadelphia.

• Bill Campbell became Boston's first free-agent signing on November 6, 1976. He received a five-year deal totaling $1 million. He said of the deal, "No one's worth that, but if they want to pay me, I'm certainly not going to turn it down."

• The Boston Red Sox scored only nine runs in the entire 1918 World Series. This total is the fewest runs by the winning team in World Series history.

Derek Lowe's no-hitter against the Tampa Bay Devil Rays in 2002 was the first no-no at Fenway Park in four decades. Lowe embodied the "cowboy up" mantra that fueled the Red Sox in 2003 and 2004.

TOPPS COLLECTORS' SERIES

ALL-TIME RECORD HOLDER

TED WILLIAMS
BOSTON RED SOX

According to the fun fact on the back of this Topps sports card, Ted Williams is the oldest player to win the batting crown, doing so at the age of 40 in 1958 with a .328 average.

# 2003

"**I** HAD THE GREATEST pitcher in the game on the mound," said manager Grady Little of his decision to leave Pedro Martinez in the game in the eighth inning of Game 7 of the ALCS vs. the Yankees.

Too bad, because the Red Sox had a very good top-of-the rotation staff of Martinez, Derek Lowe, and Tim Wakefield and a fierce lineup, which produced a whopping 961 runs. They had the AL batting champion, Bill Mueller, whose .326 average edged Manny Ramirez by a point. Yet, they still finished second to New York.

They roared back from a two-game deficit to Oakland in the ALDS and won in five games thanks to clutch pitching by Lowe, setting the stage for … drum roll … the Yankees.

It was a dramatic series even before Game 7. Typical Yankee-Red Sox nastiness broke out in Game 3 at Fenway. Martinez dropped 72-year-old Yanks coach Don Zimmer to the field after Zimmer stormed out of the dugout to protest a pitch thrown at Karim Garcia's head. In the ninth, the game ended with Yankee reliever Jeff Nelson getting into a fight with a Fenway ground crew employee.

Still, the Red Sox were two innings away from going to the World Series. In the eighth inning, they led the Yankees 5–2 until Martinez allowed three runs to tie the game. Three innings later, Yankees third baseman Aaron Boone slugged a walk-off homer.

The calm, mild-mannered Bill Mueller played a solid third base for the Red Sox in 2003 and quietly won the American League batting title. Mueller contributed to a lineup that was one of the most exciting baseball had seen.

Manager Grady Little (left) and pitcher Derek Lowe (right) shake hands after a stellar outing from Lowe in 2003. D-Lowe was a jack-of-all-trades in Boston. He saved a league-leading 42 games as a closer in 2000 and won 21 games as a starter in 2001.

# 2004

**T**ERRY FRANCONA replaced Grady Little soon after the 2003 ALCS, knowing the enormity of the task ahead of him. "I knew where the team had to go," said Francona. "We had to win the World Series."

Francona didn't disappoint. Newcomer Curt Schilling won 21 games. Keith Foulke was a dominating closer. David Ortiz and Manny Ramirez established themselves as the toughest middle of the order in baseball. Johnny Damon was a master igniter of a mashing offense that led Boston to a wild-card berth with 98 wins, three less than the first-place Yankees.

But this team's greatness will be forever proven by the 2004 American League Championship Series against the Yankees. They were down three games to none and behind in the fourth game 4–3 in the bottom of the ninth. That's when Dave Roberts stole a base to ignite the rally that led to four straight Boston wins against the Yanks, who suffered the worse collapse in baseball playoff history. "I just knew I had to do something dramatic. I was going to go, and I knew I had to get there," recalled Roberts.

Amazingly, after losing three games to New York, the 2004 Boston Red Sox won a remarkable eight games in a row, finally breaking the 86-year-old "Curse of the Bambino." They swept the St. Louis Cardinals to win the World Series trophy, bringing joyful tears to many a Red Sox fan.

**Above:** David Ortiz (left) and Manny Ramirez (right) douse themselves with champagne after clinching a playoff spot in September 2004. Just ask any opposing pitcher in the league what was the most dangerous 1-2 punch in all of baseball, and the answer was almost always Ortiz and Ramirez.

**Right:** Pitcher Bronson Arroyo was one of the heroes of the 2004 Red Sox world championship team. The 61 on his autographed ball refers to his Cincinnati Reds' jersey number. The Red Sox traded him to the Reds in 2006.

WS 04 Champs

61

# THEY WON OUR HEARTS

WADE BOGGS ONCE said about dealing with greatness, "You never allow yourself to think, 'I'm great.' You stack one season up on the next one. You keep going and play the game at the highest level you can for as long as you can. You never think 'I've done it all.' Never think that. At the end, someone thinks you're great. That's pretty neat."

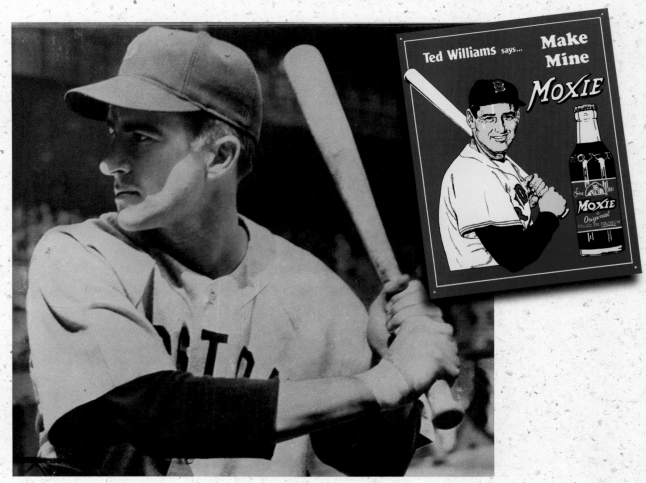

**Right:** Bobby Doerr was "the silent captain of the Red Sox" in the late '30s and early '40s. His quiet determination and professionalism on the field drew the high respect from both his teammates and opponents.

**Right Center:** Moxie is a carbonated beverage that was created in 1876 and first sold as medicine. Some claim that it is America's first mass-produced soft drink. It was not only endorsed by Ted Williams, who said it gave him extra pep, but it also became Maine's official state soft drink in 2005.

**Opposite Page:** Pedro Martinez walks back to the Red Sox dugout. During this April 8, 2001, game at Fenway against the Tampa Bay Devil Rays, he struck out 16 batters in eight innings of work.

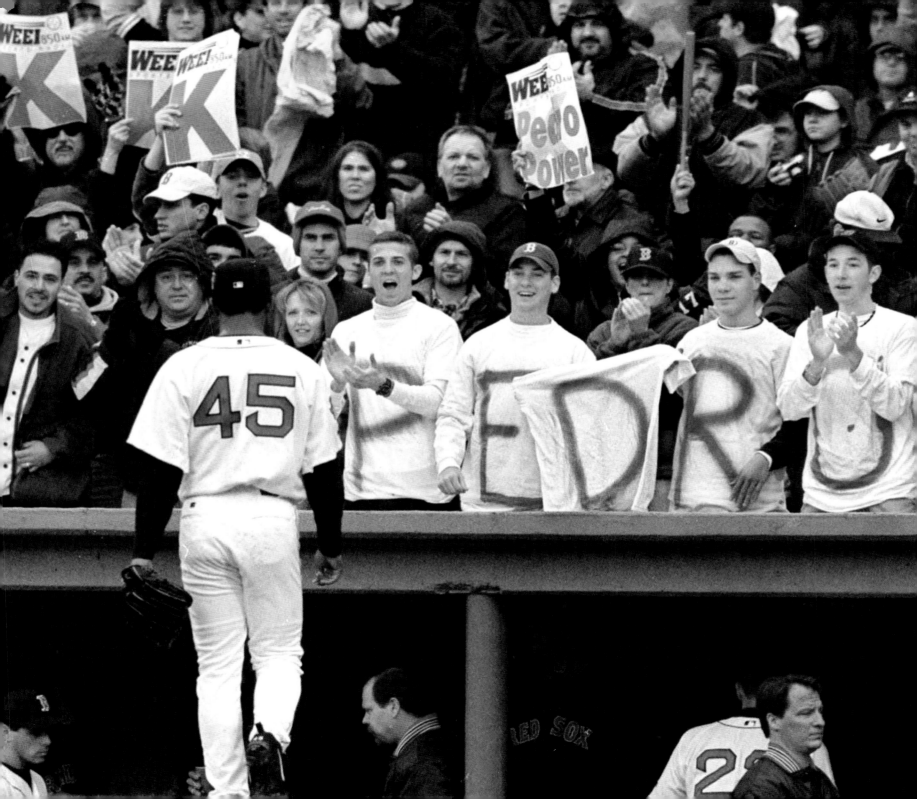

# CY YOUNG
## (1901–1908)

**H**E WAS SO GOOD that they named an award after him. Cy Young, the all-time wins leader with 511, became synonymous with greatness on the mound.

The 6'2", 200-pound right-hander, Boston baseball's first superstar, was truly the first great pitcher, combining guile, trickery, and incredible control. His famous quote was "Pitchers, like poets, are born, not made." Spending eight of his 22 seasons with the Boston Americans and Red Sox, Young was the whole show in Beantown in the early 1900s. In 1901, he won the pitching Triple Crown with 33 wins, a 1.62 ERA, and 158 strikeouts.

The modern-day fan, often irritated by the time pitchers take between pitches, would have loved Young, who worked quickly. He didn't even warm up between innings, feeling he'd waste his best stuff. Young could pitch all day, any day. He averaged 341 innings per season for the Red Sox!

**Right:** Young was born Denton True Young. His nickname is short for "Cyclone." Some say he got his nickname because he twisted his body so quickly during his windup that he resembled a cyclone.
**Far Right:** The Bradford Museum Collection has officially retired this Cy Young Tankard Baseball Legend Mug. This is the third in the Legends series and titled "Cy Young: The Perfect Game."

# JIMMY COLLINS
## (1901–1907)

Jimmy Collins, shown in this postcard, was such a whiz at third base that sportswriters called him "a magician with a glove." Some sports historians even claim that he was the best defensive third baseman before Brooks Robinson.

**H**E LED BOSTON to its first World Series title in 1903 as player-manager. His team then took the AL pennant in 1904, the year there was no World Series.

In an era with far more bunts than today, Collins was considered a pioneer of third base play. He mastered the art of coming in, barehanding the ball, and throwing runners out. Eventually, few batters tried bunting Collins's way. He was also one of the first third basemen to run down pop flies along the third base line.

Collins was a marvelous manager as well. His instincts helped avert a Pittsburgh rally with the Americans up 3–0 in the clinching game of the 1903 World Series. Collins noticed that a Pirates runner had taken a big lead off second base, so he gave a sign to the catcher, who faked a throw to second and threw down to Collins at third. Collins tagged out the breaking runner for the second out. Honus Wagner then struck out, ending the series. Collins was hailed as a genius.

# TRIS SPEAKER
## (1907–1915)

LEGEND HAS IT that Tris Speaker played center field no more than 40 feet behind the infield. He was able to catch bloopers and throw out runners in the infield. He also recorded unassisted double plays in which he'd catch a ball and then race to the bag to beat the runner who was stranded off second base. He had no problems running back on balls, and he theorized to sportswriter Bob Broeg, "I learned early that I could save more games trying to cut off some of those singles than I could by having a few extra-base hits go over my head."

He was a show in and of himself, especially in 1912, when the new Fenway Park opened. The fans flocked to see Speaker play and Smoky Joe Wood pitch. Speaker hit .383 and was spectacular on defense. Born in Hubbard City, Texas, he was a .345 career hitter.

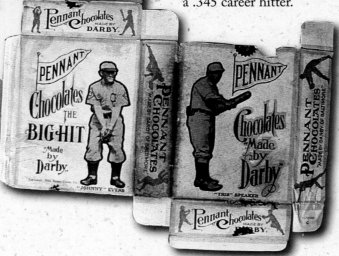

**Above:** While playing football, Speaker injured his left arm so badly that his doctors wanted to amputate it. He refused and later became one of the greatest center fielders. In fact, he became the seventh member of the Baseball Hall of Fame.

**Right:** Tris Speaker and Johnny Evers of the Chicago Cubs are featured on this Darby chocolate box, which was sold around 1909.

# SMOKY JOE WOOD
## (1908–1915)

**S**MOKY JOE WOOD was the hardest thrower of his era, causing his nemesis/pitching competitor Walter Johnson to remark, "Can I throw harder than Joe Wood? Listen, mister, no man alive can throw any harder than Smoky Joe Wood."

Fireballer Wood had the greatest single season for a pitcher in Red Sox history— 34–5 (with a 1.91 ERA and 10 shutouts) in 1912. He added a 3–1 record in that year's World Series, including the clinching game in an eight-game series, besting the great Christy Mathewson of the New York Giants.

The highlight of his career might have been at Fenway on September 6, 1912, vs. Walter Johnson. In that classic, Wood, 22 years old at the time, beat Johnson 1–0. At a reunion of the greatest Red Sox players at Fenway a year before his death in 1985, Wood, then 95 years old, recalled, "That was the only game I remember at Fenway Park or anywhere else for that matter. The fans were practically sitting along the first base line and the third base line."

Nicknamed "Smoky" for the furious fastballs he blew by hitters, Joe Wood won three games for the Red Sox during the 1912 World Series en route to being recognized as one of the greatest pitchers of all time. Wood was regarded as a true class act by those who knew him.

# I'LL TAKE IT IN LEATHER, PLEASE

**H**ALL OF FAMER Tris Speaker played such a shallow center field that he was often able to sneak behind second base and pick off a runner. It would be difficult to argue against Speaker as the best defensive player in Red Sox history. Moreover, he joined Duffy Lewis and Harry Hooper as one of the best defensive Red Sox outfields.

But there are certainly other Red Sox players to consider for their defensive skills. Under the category of "special," it was hard to top center fielder Dominic DiMaggio. Someone who saw them all, except Speaker, was Mr. Red Sox, Johnny Pesky, a pretty fair shortstop himself in the '40s and '50s. "Dominic never made a mistake," said Pesky. "Never threw to the wrong base. Day in and day out the best."

Pesky also called Bobby Doerr "the best second baseman we ever had." And on catcher Carlton Fisk he said, "by far the best. The best at throwing out runners and handling a pitching staff."

When Jimmy Piersall replaced Dom DiMaggio in center, Ted Williams called him "the best center fielder I've ever seen."

Bobby Doerr scoops up a ground ball with his bare hand. Amazingly, he once handled 414 chances in a row without an error.

Right fielder Dwight Evans won eight Gold
Gloves and had one of the strongest arms of
his era. "I'd say Yaz, Evans, Dominic, and Fred
Lynn were the perfect outfielders," Pesky said.

While DiMaggio made it look effortless,
first baseman George "Boomer" Scott was as
flashy with the glove as any first baseman who
ever played; his flare for scooping bad throws
was unmatched. Carl Yastrzemski once commented on Scott, "In my 23 years in baseball,
I have never seen a better defensive player.
I have never seen a player with the baseball
instincts of Scotty."

A seven-time Gold Glove winner himself,
Yastrzemski was undoubtedly the best defensive left fielder the Red Sox ever had. Yaz
made an art out of playing balls off the Green
Monster and holding hitters to singles. He is
known for his great tumbling catch to preserve
a no-hitter for Billy Rohr in 1967 at Yankee
Stadium. Manager Dick Williams commented:
"I'd never seen a player who made more incredible defensive plays in 1967 than Yaz."

**Above:** Dwight Evans races across the field during
the 1975 World Series against the Cincinnati Reds.
Al Kaline is the only American League right fielder
to win more Gold Gloves than Evans.
**Left:** In 1933, Joe Cronin was a busy man. He not
only was the shortstop and manager of the Washington Senators, but he also took time to do this ad,
which featured his fielding glove. Two years later,
he took his glove to the Boston Red Sox.

REACH FIELDERS' GLOVES

No. OOW
The
Joe Cronin
Fielders' Glove

Joe Cronin
Manager and Short Stop of the
Washington "Senators."

Joe Cronin is another
player who knows what
he wants in glove con-
struction. The gloves
we made for him meet
the requirements of so
many other players that
we supply it regularly
and identify the model
by branding it with Joe's name. Made of good quality
brown grain oil-treated horsehide. Full leather lined.
Leather binding and welting. Leather laced wrist. Laced
between thumb and first finger. Hand-formed felt padding
with deep, natural pocket. "V" shaped back with strap-
and-buckle fastener. Thoroughly practical in every detail
of construction. . . . . . . . . . . . . . . . . . . . . Each $5.50

No. OOW

No. OOW
Showing Back Construction

No. DF. The Rube Walberg

# BABE RUTH
## (1914–1919)

**W**HEN HE BROKE the single-season home run record with 29 in 1919, his last season in Boston, it was evident Babe Ruth was on his way to becoming perhaps the greatest slugger the game has ever known. That didn't stop Red Sox owner Harry Frazee from selling him to the Yankees for $125,000 and a $300,000 loan to help pay the mortgage on Fenway Park.

Criticized heavily for the sale, Frazee released a statement to the press that said, among other unflattering things, "While Ruth is the greatest hitter that the game has seen, he is likewise one of the most inconsiderate men that ever wore a baseball uniform."

Ruth would go on to legendary status with the Yankees, but his Red Sox career was an eye-opener as well. As a dominant left-handed pitcher for the Red Sox, he went 89–46 and owned a string of $29\frac{2}{3}$ scoreless innings in the World Series, a record until Whitey Ford broke it with the Yankees in the 1960s. His departure and the 86-year drought between championships was dubbed, by *Boston Globe* columnist Dan Shaughnessy, "The Curse of the Bambino."

**Above:** George Herman Ruth is shown here as a member of the Boston Red Sox. "The Babe" was larger than life both on the field and off.
**Left:** As the button shows, the Babe played six memorable seasons for the Red Sox.

# LEFTY GROVE
## (1934–1941)

**B**Y THE TIME 1941 rolled around, Lefty Grove, then 41, was at the end of a glorious career. "He was still quite a show every time he pitched," Dom DiMaggio remembered. "For as many things that happened in that incredible year of 1941, Lefty getting his 300th win [on July 26] was right up there with all of it. He was so respected. Such a classy individual. We were all proud to have played with him."

Grove's best seasons were with the Philadelphia A's, where he was on two championship teams and won 31 games in 1931. He was traded to the Red Sox in 1933 and won 105 games with Boston. He earned 20 wins only once with Boston, in 1935. Yet he won enough to be among the team's winningest lefties. He had a 55–17 record at Fenway.

In 1983, Joe Cronin was asked to name his all-time Red Sox team. He named Grove as his left-handed pitcher. "He was great at getting the first man out in ninth-inning situations when the Sox were protecting a one-run lead," Cronin told *The Boston Globe*. "He developed a great curveball while he was with Boston. But he came up with a sore arm and just barely won his 300th game at Fenway before calling it quits."

Hall of Famer Lefty Grove was a staple of the Red Sox rotation during the 1930s. Grove finished his career with 300 wins and is considered one of the best left-handed pitchers of all time.

# JOE CRONIN
## (1935–1945)

THERE WAS NEVER more meaning to the phrase "Baseball was his life" than as it applied to No. 4—Joe Cronin. The all-time greatest Red Sox shortstop wound up with a career .301 average in 20 seasons in the majors. He also became a manager for both the Washington Senators and the Red Sox, amassing a 1,236–1,055 record. He won two American League championships: with the Senators in 1933 and with the Red Sox in 1946. He became Boston's general manager and also served as the American League president from 1959 to 1973.

Cronin did his part to promote the Red Sox–Yankees rivalry. On May 30, 1938, the first game of a Memorial Day double-header at Yankee Stadium with an estimated 84,000 fans on hand, Cronin and Yankee curmudgeon Jake Powell engaged in quite an altercation. It started on the field and spilled over into the area leading to the clubhouses.

**Above:** Cronin often leaped high in the air while playing shortstop. Because of both his glove and his bat, he was selected to seven All-Star teams.

# JIMMIE FOXX
## (1936–1942)

THIS HALL OF FAME first baseman spent six-and-a-half unforgettable seasons of his 20-year career with the Red Sox. He was a powerful right-handed hitter.

"We played an exhibition game against Cincinnati in 1941 and beyond the left-field fence, and what seemed to be a half mile away, was another fence in front of a Laundromat," said his former Red Sox roommate, Dom DiMaggio. "The bases were loaded, the count was 3-2. Foxx hit one…and I just stopped between second and third to watch it. It landed on top of the roof of the Laundromat."

In 1938, "Double X" hit 50 homers (which stood as the all-time Red Sox record until David Ortiz hit 54 in 2006) with 175 RBI and a .349 average (.405 with 35 homers at Fenway) to take the American league MVP award, his first of three. He followed that in 1939 with a .360 average and 35 homers. The nine-time All-Star finished with a .325 career average, 534 homers, 1,922 RBI, and two World Series rings.

Jimmie Foxx watches one of his 534 career home runs leave the yard. Considered one of the best right-handed hitters of all time, Foxx enjoyed one of the greatest seasons ever by a Red Sox in 1938.

# A BRIEF STINT IN BOSTON

THROUGHOUT RED SOX HISTORY, the team has signed or traded for players who had excellent, if not Hall of Fame, careers for other teams and came to Boston for short stints at the ends of their careers.

Orlando Cepeda, who earned his Hall of Fame plaque mostly with the Giants and Cardinals, was Boston's first designated hitter in 1973. Tony Perez forged his Hall of Fame career with the Big Red Machine Cincinnati Reds, but he signed with the Red Sox as a free agent in 1980 and, at age 39, knocked in 105 runs and hit 25 homers.

Hall of Fame shortstop Luis Aparicio had lost a step by the time he came to Boston in 1971. Nevertheless, he spent his final three seasons as Boston's starting shortstop. Rickey Henderson, the all-time stolen base leader (1,406) and a surefire first-ballot Hall of Famer, spent the 2002 season, his next-to-last in the majors, with the Red Sox.

Andre Dawson, who hit 438 homers and knocked in 1,509 runs, spent two seasons with the Red Sox as a DH at age 38 and 39 before finishing his career with the Florida Marlins. Making a huge contribution as a catcher with a young Red Sox pitching staff in 1967 was Elston Howard, the long-time Yankee.

Juan Marichal, Ferguson Jenkins, and Tom Seaver were among many Hall of Famers who became part of Red Sox history.

**Above:** Tony Perez manned the first base bag at Fenway Park from 1980 to 1982. This Hall of Fame first baseman was one of the great run producers of his era and won the honorable Lou Gehrig Memorial Award in 1980.

**Right:** Orlando Cepeda helped make history for and against the Boston Red Sox. Cepeda was a star on the Cardinals 1967 World Series team that ultimately ended the Impossible Dream season. He also became the Red Sox' first designated hitter in 1973 on his way to the Hall of Fame. Notice the misspelling ("Soxs") on his button.

ORLANDO CEPEDA
RED SOXS

# BOBBY DOERR
## (1937–1944, 1946–1951)

THOSE WHO PLAYED with him recall his quiet strength. He was a rock of a man, as steady and dependable as any ballplayer who ever put on the uniform. To put it in modern terms, he was Cal Ripken-like. You knew what you were getting every day.

"When I played, we didn't have a captain," Ted Williams told *The Boston Globe* shortly after Doerr was voted into the Hall of Fame by the Veterans' Committee in 1986. "But Bobby was the silent captain. He was the guy I felt was the solidifier here."

Discovered along with Ted Williams by Eddie Collins on a scouting trip to Southern California, Doerr joined the Red Sox in 1937 at age 19. Over his 14-year career with the Red Sox, Doerr was as smooth as silk around the second base bag. He hit .288 for his career, had six 100-RBI seasons, and made nine All-Star teams. He hit for the cycle (a single, a double, a triple, and a home run) on May 13, 1947, against Chicago, becoming the only player in team history to accomplish the feat twice. He also cycled on May 17, 1944, against St. Louis.

Bobby Doerr was a brilliant second baseman who played his entire 14-year career with the Boston Red Sox. The team retired his jersey number (1) in 1988.

# TED WILLIAMS
## (1939–1942, 1946–1960)

**T**HE GREATEST HITTER there ever was, Ted Williams is said to be able to read the label of a pitched ball from home plate. He was such an expert hitter that he could also detect, to a fraction of an ounce, incongruity in the weight of a bat.

Williams retired with a .344 career average and was the last man to hit .400 for a season (.406 in 1941). He accomplished this feat despite refusing to protect his .400 average by sitting out the last day of the season. He was 6-for-8 in that doubleheader. And he won the Triple Crown twice.

Williams was also considered an expert naval war pilot and angler. More importantly, he single-handedly began the Jimmy Fund, the successful fund-raising arm of the Dana Farber Cancer Institute, and led the charge for baseball to recognize the contributions of Negro League players.

One of the most memorable moments in baseball history was when Williams slugged his 521st home run in his last at-bat on September 26, 1960. "The Splendid Splinter" took a Jack Fisher fastball and sent it into the right-field bleachers.

"What a great teammate," said Johnny Pesky. "He kidded us little guys, but he understood we got on base so he could drive us in and he always appreciated that."

Ted Williams poses for a photograph while wielding his most dangerous weapon: a baseball bat. Williams was inducted into the Baseball Hall of Fame in 1966.

# DOMINIC DIMAGGIO
## (1940–1942, 1946–1953)

THE "LITTLE PROFESSOR" is one of the best top-of-the-order players and defenders of all-time. Asked what he was most proud of in his career, he replied, "I made it to the major leagues wearing glasses. That opened the floodgates for many other players who wore glasses, who like me, had been told they'd never make it."

He was best known, along with Johnny Pesky, as Ted Williams's table-setter, and DiMaggio never ran away from the moniker. Nor did he run away from the fact that he was the brother of a living legend—Joe DiMaggio. As if it were something that ran in the family, DiMaggio to this day holds the Red Sox record for the longest hitting streak—34 games in 1949.

"I'm a little amazed that some 50 years later, it's still the record," DiMaggio said. "Doesn't compare to Joe's, but Joe and Ted, they were one-of-a-kind. I was so lucky to have been on a team with so many great players. We had a ball."

**Top Left:** This Dom DiMaggio autographed baseball is another historic piece of memorabilia that's worth a pretty penny.
**Above:** Notice anything unusual about this picture? Dom DiMaggio was one of the first major-leaguers to wear eyeglasses while playing. Dom was affectionately nicknamed "The Little Professor" due to his glasses and 5'9" stature.

# MEL PARNELL
## (1947–1956)

**Y**OU MIGHT SAY Mel Parnell shattered the myth that lefties couldn't win at Fenway. In a ballpark where big right-handed hitters salivated at seeing a lefty, nobody liked facing this southpaw.

Parnell was raised in New Orleans. He flourished at Fenway, racking up 71 career wins in Boston, with a 123–75 overall record in 10 seasons. He won 25 in 1949.

"For me the strategy was simple," Parnell said. "You had to pitch inside to right-handed hitters so they couldn't extend their arms and take you deep. I changed the way I pitched from the minors to the majors when I saw the ballpark. In the minors I threw mostly fastballs, but when I started pitching at Fenway, I threw mostly curves and sliders because I wanted the movement on the ball to ride in on a right-handed hitter and stay low. I never nibbled outside because if I missed, it would be over the plate."

Mel Parnell enjoyed his best season in 1949. The southpaw recorded a 25–7 record with a 2.77 ERA and 27 complete games. He also was the starting pitcher in that year's All-Star Game.

# CARL
## YASTRZEMSKI
### (1961–1983)

**T**HE MAN THEY called "Yaz" put together what many consider the greatest post World War II season ever by a Red Sox player. In 1967, he captured the Triple Crown for the "Impossible Dream" Red Sox with a .326 batting average, 44 home runs, and 121 RBI. He won the MVP award for his amazing performance.

A seven-time Gold Glove winner in left field, Yaz was known for his unique batting stance with hands high and bat cocked above his head. At the end of the 1967 season, Yaz went 23-for-44 (.523), slugged five homers, and picked up 16 RBI as the Red Sox won 8 of 12 final games to win the pennant.

Yastrzemski, who played 23 seasons, amassed 452 homers and 3,419 hits. He was one of the first baseball players to use an off-season work-out regimen, which showed up in his longevity. "I never expected to play that long," said Yaz. "I never expected most of the things that happened to me."

**Far Right:** Carl Yastrzemski played his entire major-league career with the Boston Red Sox, all 23 seasons. An 18-time All-Star, Yaz was inducted into the Baseball Hall of Fame in 1989.

**Right:** If you used this ticket to get into Fenway in 1979, you would have seen Yaz get his 3,000 hit, which put him into an elite group of hitters.

# WILLIAMS vs. YAZ

**T**ED WILLIAMS'S .406 season in 1941 and Carl Yastrzemski's Triple Crown season in 1967 are two of the greatest feats in baseball history. Neither one has been matched to date.

Hitting .406 in the modern age is to baseball what Wilt Chamberlain's 100-point game is to the NBA, what *Titanic* is to the box office, and what Nixon's 1972 landslide victory was to presidential elections. It has never been topped, nor is it likely it ever will be.

Nomar Garciaparra approached the feat in 2000, flirting with the .400 mark for much of the year but ultimately falling to .372 at year's end. Hitting .400 requires that streaks must be extended, slumps must be limited, and injuries must be nonfactors. There have been countless other megastars who have burst onto the scene with record-breaking ability since 1941, but hitting over .400 is the ultimate measure of greatness in the sport of baseball. It may never be seen again.

Just as Teddy Ballgame conquered the baseball landscape in 1941, the next definitive Red Sox legend, Carl Yastrzemski, dominated America's pastime in 1967. His Triple Crown performance—leading the league in batting average, home runs, and runs batted

When Ted Williams won the batting championship in 1958, he became the oldest player in baseball history to win the title. "The Kid" had turned 40.

in—has not been matched in 40 years, adding to Yaz's historic legacy. Being the best in three categories as a hitter is quite an accomplishment. Yaz hit .326 with 44 homers and 121 runs batted in, earning him MVP honors.

In today's era, many power hitters lead the league in the home run and RBI categories but don't have the league-leading batting average. A Triple Crown achievement puts you head and shoulders above your peers, and Carl Yastrzemski was just that, leading the hometown team to the World Series. If his feat is ever matched, it would have to be by a player the caliber of the legendary Yaz.

The last word from Johnny Pesky, who played with Ted and managed Yaz: "I was in awe of so many things that Ted did and obviously nobody's ever hit .400 since, but I always thought the year Yaz had in '67 was the best I've ever seen."

**Above:** This 1964 Topps All-Star coin of Carl Yastrzemski is #26 of a 120-coin set. The back of the coin notes that he was the American League's batting champ in 1963.
**Right:** Yaz saw many of his hits fly over Fenway's right-field wall. In addition, he is the Red Sox leader in career RBI, runs, hits, singles, doubles, total bases, and games played.

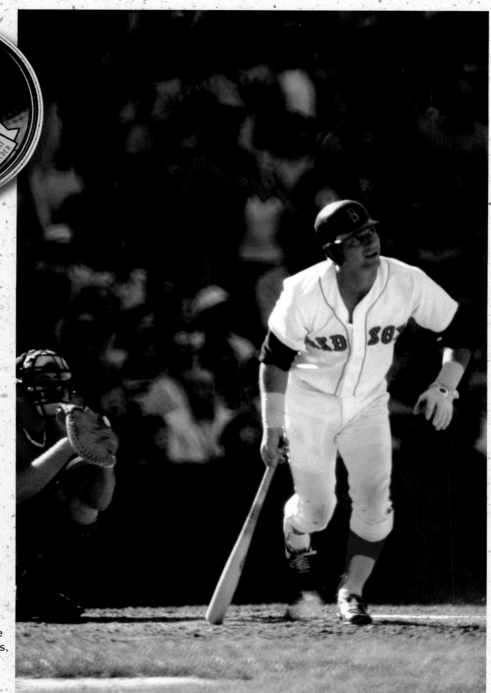

# CARLTON FISK
## (1969, 1971–1980)

**F**ISK'S JERSEY NUMBER is one of five retired Red Sox numbers hung on the right-field facade at Fenway Park. This Hall of Fame catcher is also the pride of Charlestown, New Hampshire. He caught more games (2,226) than any catcher in baseball history. He had two careers within one that could be split virtually in half: 1969–1980 with the Boston Red Sox and 1981–1993 with the Chicago White Sox. He amassed 376 homers, went to 11 All-Star Games (seven with Boston), and caught until he was 45 years old, thanks to a disciplined weight-lifting regimen.

"I felt like I just wanted to play forever. As long as I felt strong and felt I could do the job and help the team, I thought I could play," Fisk said.

He is famous for his jumping wave at his walk-off 12th-inning homer in Game 6 of the 1975 World Series, which gave the Red Sox a 7–6 win and forced a Game 7. One of the most competitive Red Sox players ever, he once fought with Yankee backstop Thurman Munson, not only in collisions on the field but also for the right to be called the best catcher the American League had to offer.

Moments after "The Wave," an ecstatic Carlton Fisk is greeted by his teammates as he crosses home plate. Fisk's walk-off home run in the 12th inning of Game 6 during the 1975 World Series is one of the most enduring moments in Red Sox history.

# LUIS TIANT
## (1971–1978)

**W**HEN HE PITCHED in the late 1970s, there was electricity in the air. Known for turning his body almost completely to second base before delivering the pitch, Luis Tiant had one of the most deceptive deliveries in baseball history. Little kids were twirling around like *El Tiante* throughout New England.

"If a man put a gun to my head and said I'm going to pull the trigger if you lose this game, I'd want Luis Tiant to pitch that game," said former Red Sox manager Darrell Johnson.

Tiant is known for his 1.60 ERA with the Cleveland Indians in 1968, and he also threw four consecutive shutouts that season. But he was also a big-game pitcher. He earned three 20-win seasons with the Red Sox over his eight years in Boston.

**Above:** Luis Tiant won 122 games for the Red Sox in his Hall of Fame-worthy career. From 1973 through 1976, he averaged 20 wins a year.
**Left:** A classic Boston Red Sox logo pin atop a glove and two baseball bats is a great item for a member of Red Sox Nation.

# DWIGHT EVANS
## (1972–1990)

**K**NOWN AS "DEWEY," Evans could have been called "The Rifleman" because of his incredible arm in right field. He was once pegged by Red Sox legend Johnny Pesky as "the perfect outfielder."

Evans took great pride in his fielding, which produced eight Gold Gloves. Yet he also hit 385 career home runs and knocked in 1,384 runs, becoming a feared hitter. Evans was lost at the plate over the first nine years of his career, only twice hitting 20 or more homers before he discovered hitting coach Walt Hriniak. Evans hit more than 20 homers nine times from 1981 on.

Who can forget the stellar 11th-inning catch he made to rob Cincinnati Reds second baseman Joe Morgan of a home run (and then doubled up Ken Griffey at first base)? That incredible grab allowed Carlton Fisk a chance for his unforgettable 12th-inning walk-off homer in Game 6 of the 1975 World Series. Reds manager Sparky Anderson called it "the greatest catch I've ever seen."

Only Carl Yastrzemski played more games for the Red Sox than Dwight Evans, who appeared in more than 2,500 games during his 19 years with the team.

# JIM RICE
## (1974–1989)

**O**NE OF THE TOP sluggers of the 1980s, Jim Rice wants to be remembered for only this: "That I played the game hard every day. That I went out there when I was hurt. That I never let my teammates down and that I helped win games. That's all."

Rice was like Ted Williams in that he never warmed up to the members of the Fourth Estate. In fact, Rice would never be around for media sound bites after he'd gone 4-for-4 or won a game. But if he made an error or struck out with the bases loaded, Rice would be at his locker waiting for the sports media so he could place the blame on himself.

Because of his team-first attitude, Rice was considered one of the great teammates in Red Sox history. And for the decade of the 1980s, there wasn't anyone better in the American League. He was finally elected to the Hall of Fame in 2009.

**Far Left:** Jim Rice was one of baseball's most imposing batters in his day. Rice now works as a Red Sox analyst on NESN.
**Left:** Wilson manufactured this Jim Rice-autographed baseball glove. Rice won the American League MVP Award in 1978 and played his entire career in a Red Sox jersey.

# FISK vs. VARITEK

HERE ARE TWO catchers who earned the respect of their pitching staffs and managers in the eras in which they played. "Is Carlton Fisk or Jason Varitek better defensively?" isn't an easy question to answer.

We did manage to find a player—NESN color analyst Jerry Remy—who played with Fisk and who has broadcast all of Varitek's Boston games. Thus, he has firsthand knowledge of both catchers.

"We used to call Fisk 'Magic' because he was just special back there," Remy recalls. "He had soft hands, and for a big guy he was so athletic. He had an excellent, strong, and accurate throwing arm, and baserunners thought twice about stealing on him. Overall, I would say Fisk was the better receiver. Fisk is in the Hall of Fame for a reason. I think Jason is superb with the pitchers, and he has a lot more information at his fingertips than Fisk did. Back then you had an advance scouting report and your memory. Now, you have everything broken down, and to Jason's credit he uses that information to his advantage."

In recent years when Varitek has gone down to injury, the Red Sox pitching staff has seemed lost at times. Varitek has been their guiding light in terms of pitch selection. Fisk, too, was hands on. As Remy points out, "He

**Left:** Carlton Fisk, a Gold Glove catcher, holds the record for the most games caught—2,226. When he was inducted into the Hall of Fame, he chose the Red Sox cap for his plaque.
**Right:** Red Sox catcher Jason Varitek tags out Mike Napoli of the Los Angeles Angels of Anaheim. Varitek leads by example and has earned the respect of his teammates and his opponents alike.
**Upper Right:** This cartoon poster of Jason Varitek is a limited-edition print. If there's one thing his teammates will say about him, it's that he does not have a big head.

wasn't afraid to let the pitcher know exactly how he felt." Varitek, too, is a leader and wears the "C" that represents his role as team captain.

In Fisk's era, pitchers like Luis Tiant were workhorses. If the pitch count rose well past 100, it wasn't as big of an issue as it has become in Varitek's time. Both, according to Remy, were good handlers of their respective pitching staffs. But in terms of pure, raw ability, Fisk comes out on top in this argument.

# FRED LYNN
## (1974–1980)

Fred Lynn races out of the batter's box during a Red Sox game in 1978. Lynn and fellow outfielder Jim Rice both debuted in 1974 and were nicknamed the "Gold Dust Twins" because of their amazing combined talents.

**I**F FRED LYNN made one drastic mistake in his career, it was wanting to be traded out of Boston after the 1980 season to be close to his Southern California home. "I think I would have put up pretty impressive career numbers if I'd played at Fenway throughout my career," Lynn said.

A graceful, gliding player and a tremendous defensive center fielder, Lynn had a perfect swing. Perfect for Fenway. He had excellent power to the gaps, and he made baseball look easy. He hit .347 for his career at Fenway with an OPS (slugging percentage plus on-base percentage) of a whopping 1.021.

He broke onto the scene in 1975 and became the first player to win the Rookie of the Year and MVP awards in the same season. He also won his first of four Gold Gloves and made his first of nine consecutive All-Star teams.

# WADE BOGGS
## (1982–1992)

**W**ADE BOGGS could wait until the last possible instant to hit a baseball—a testament to his incredible reflexes and hitting eye. He used to talk about hitting the top of the ball to create a desired spin. He didn't hit homers like Ted Williams or steal bases like Tris Speaker. Although he had many quirks and superstitions, Boggs was a hitting phenomenon.

"I'm the luckiest man in baseball," said Boggs, inducted into the Hall of Fame in 2005. "Fenway Park was made for me. I loved hitting the ball the other way, and the other way for me at Fenway was a base hit."

Boggs won five batting titles and had 200 hits for an American League-record seven consecutive years. After falling to .259 in 1992, his final year in Boston, Boggs won two Gold Gloves and batted over .300 four times for the New York Yankees.

He ate chicken prior to every game and was thus pegged with the nickname "Chicken Man" by Jim Rice. Boggs had 150 ground balls hit to him every day by Johnny Pesky, took the field at precisely 7:17 P.M. and drew the Hebrew "Chai" emblem in the batter's box prior to every at-bat.

**Above:** Hall of Fame third baseman Wade Boggs does what he did best: put the ball into play. Boggs hit .357 in 1986, leading Boston to its only World Series appearance of the decade.
**Right:** Wade Boggs was a pure hitter and a great third baseman for the Red Sox in his day. Here is Boggs's autographed 2005 Hall of Fame ball.

# ROGER CLEMENS
## (1984–1996)

**Y**EARS LATER HE would say about his successful and sometimes tumultuous times in Boston, "There's no better place to play baseball." Though he won championships in New York, two Cy Young Awards in Toronto, and pitched in his hometown of Houston, Roger Clemens will be best remembered for what he accomplished while wearing a Red Sox cap.

At the center of his amazing career are a pair of 20-strikeout games, one in 1986 against the Seattle Mariners and one ten years later in 1996 against the Detroit Tigers. He's tied with Cy Young as the all-time Red Sox victory leader with 192. Clemens never won a championship with the Red Sox, but his 1986 season in which he went 24–4 and took home Cy Young and MVP honors is unforgettable.

"Roger Clemens made pitching relevant again in Boston," said former Red Sox general manager Lou Gorman.

Clemens is nicknamed "The Rocket" because of his blazing fastball. He has won the Cy Young Award a record seven times.

# MO VAUGHN
## (1991–1998)

EASILY THE MOST popular Red Sox player of the 1990s, Mo Vaughn championed causes for inner-city kids, was a leader in the clubhouse, and spoke his mind like no other Red Sox player. Former Seton Hall and Red Sox teammate John Valentin once said of Vaughn, "Let me tell you this. There is nobody—nobody—I'd rather have up there for us. You can talk [Ken] Griffey, [Barry] Bonds, [Mark] McGwire, and I don't care. Nobody has a bigger heart than Mo."

Beating out Cleveland's Albert Belle for the 1995 MVP, he hit long, majestic home runs. His beautiful in-and-out swing fit Fenway perfectly. He once hit three homers in a game against the Yanks and nearly became the first to hit one out of old Memorial Stadium in Baltimore.

He hit 230 homers in less than eight seasons in Boston with more than 700 RBI. Six times in his career he drove in more than 100 runs, and six times he hit 30 or more homers.

**Above:** This 1991 Fleer update card shows Mo Vaughn slugging a home run during his rookie season.
**Left:** Here Vaughn is safe as he slides into home under Oakland A's catcher Terry Steinbach in 1996. Vaughn thrived during his eight seasons in Boston.

# THE ROCKET vs. PEDRO

IN MAJOR-LEAGUE baseball you have your good pitchers, you have your great pitchers, and then you have "The Rocket" and Pedro—two names that will be mentioned at the start of any debate about classic Red Sox hurlers.

So who's better?

Clemens is a product of the stellar Red Sox farm system of the early 1980s. He blasted his way onto the scene in 1984 as one of the hardest throwers in all of baseball. Capturing the hearts and minds of Red Sox fans everywhere, Clemens showcased his power, overmatching opposing batters.

Then, in 1986, Clemens truly arrived. That year, the sports world stood in awe as the 23-year-old righty fanned batter after batter throughout the season. Clemens won the league's MVP and Cy Young awards in 1986, leading the Red Sox to the World Series. It is a rare and remarkable feat for a pitcher to be awarded the MVP. Then, over the course of the next ten years, Clemens would rack up 192 Red Sox victories (tying Cy Young's franchise record) and three Cy Young awards en route to setting the Red Sox franchise record for strikeouts.

**Top Center:** Shown on this pin as a young Rocket, Clemens has worn many jerseys in his day, but fans in Boston will forever remember Roger as a Red Sox ace.
**Above:** Here Clemens shuts out the Tigers in 1996. He was the first of his generation to reach 45 shutouts and 4,500 strikeouts.

After The Rocket departed Red Sox Nation, the Fenway faithful looked for a new pitching hero to rally behind. Enter Pedro Martinez. Starting in 1998, Pedro's repertoire dazzled opposing hitters for seven amazing seasons in Boston. In 1999, "Peedee" chalked up one of the great seasons in baseball history, finishing with a 23–4 record and a brilliant 2.07 ERA.

Thought to be out of action for Game 5 of the playoffs in Cleveland with an injury, Martinez entered the game in the 4th inning and threw six hitless innings, ensuring the Red Sox's first playoff series victory in years. In the 2004 World Series, Martinez was in rare form, winning Game 3 en route to a Red Sox sweep.

We asked former Red Sox manager Joe Morgan, Clemens's manager and Martinez's keen observer, to answer the difficult question: Who was the best?

"I'd say it this way, if they both went out with their worst stuff, Pedro would win because he had the finesse—the changeup, slider, curveball. That's the way I'd look at it. For a few years Pedro was as good as anyone I've ever seen, and I played with Bob Gibson and Warren Spahn," Morgan said.

Pedro Martinez lit up the National League during his 1999 All-Star appearance. Martinez's 1999 season was as good a year as any pitcher has ever had.

# NOMAR GARCIAPARRA
## (1996–2004)

**M**UCH LIKE FRED LYNN, Nomar Garciaparra burst onto the scene with the Red Sox with a record-setting rookie season in 1997. Garciaparra hit 30 homers and knocked in an MLB-record 98 runs from the leadoff spot.

"One of the toughest outs and best all-around hitters in the game," said Yankee shortstop Derek Jeter, commenting on the early part of Garciaparra's career. "For a pitcher, it's hard to pitch to him because he could hit bad pitches out of the ballpark."

In that way he was sort of a modern-day Roberto Clemente. Garciaparra was up there hacking, which is why in 2000 he was hitting .403 on July 20 after going 3-for-5 against the Orioles. He settled for a .372 average to win the American League batting title. He was a career .337 hitter at Fenway heading into the 2007 season.

**Left:** Nomar Garciaparra was the total package in Boston. Nomar turns a beautiful double play in the ninth inning of a 2002 game against Toronto.
**Below:** Garciaparra autographed this baseball. For a time, there was no hotter athlete in New England than Nomar. He was often compared to Ted Williams early in his career. Garciaparra will go down as one of the most popular Red Sox of all time.

# PEDRO MARTINEZ
## (1998–2004)

Although Martinez's 13-game wining streak ended against the Tampa Bay Devil Rays at Fenway, a 1–0 loss on May 6, 2000, he did strike out 17 batters.

**W**HEN DAN DUQUETTE traded pitching prospects Tony Armas, Jr., and Carl Pavano for Pedro Martinez in the winter of 1997, he finally made fans forget, at least in part, Roger Clemens. Martinez's 1999 season is commonly considered one of the greatest of the post-Word War II era—23–4 with a 2.07 ERA and 313 strikeouts.

While frequently battling with Red Sox management, Martinez amassed a 117–37 record—the best winning percentage in Red Sox history. One of his great moments came in the 1999 All-Star Game in Boston when he became the first pitcher to strike out the first four batters of a midsummer classic—Barry Larkin, Larry Walker, Sammy Sosa, and Mark McGwire.

Martinez was also very much involved in the Red Sox–Yankee rivalry, uttering, "I don't believe in damn curses. Wake up the Bambino, and have me face him. Maybe I'll drill him in the ass."

# MANNY RAMIREZ
## (2001–2008)

**O**NE OF THE GREATEST right-handed hitters, Ramirez is cut in the mold of Jimmie Foxx and Jim Rice. He ended the 2008 season with a career .314 batting average and 527 home runs. A surefire Hall of Famer, Ramirez makes hitting look easy. According to Philadelphia Phillies manager Charlie Manuel, who was Ramirez's hitting coach in the minors and with the Cleveland Indians, "He can wear out bad pitching and he can hit good pitching. It's very rare a great pitcher gets the best of Manny."

The MVP of the 2004 World Series, Ramirez was popular in Red Sox Nation. The lovable catch phrase "Manny being Manny" refers to some of the odd and unpredictable things Ramirez does, usually unwittingly, to both annoy and amuse his teammates and fan base. This phrase has become common jargon.

In 1999, Ramirez delivered a remarkable 165 RBI for the Cleveland Indians. He later signed one of the richest contracts ever— eight years, $160 million—with the Boston Red Sox prior to the 2001 season. By 2008, he wore out his welcome, and he was traded to the Dodgers.

**Above:** On October 6, 2003, in Oakland, Ramirez smacked a crucial home run (pictured) against the A's in the fifth game of the American League Division Series.
**Right:** This Manny Ramirez bobblehead is part of the "Legends of the Diamonds" series. Manny is a true baseball superstar and a future Hall of Famer.

Big Papi won the Hank Aaron Award for the top hitter in the American League for the 2005 season. Voters probably remembered this image of him slugging a three-run homer in the 2004 World Series at Fenway.

# DAVID ORTIZ
## (2003– )

**O**NE OF THE MOST beloved Red Sox players, David Ortiz is affectionately known as "Big Papi" to a legion of Red Sox fans. A designated hitter, he was signed off the Minnesota Twins' scrap heap prior to the 2003 season and has emerged as one of the most dangerous hitters in the game. His signature is the walk-off hit. In 2006, he had five of them.

"It's my job," said Ortiz of his penchant for the dramatic. "When I'm up and I can win a game, I expect to win it. If I don't, I've let the team down." Oh, and he did come through in the 2004 American League Championship Series vs. the Yankees when he had walk-off hits in Games 4 and 5 less than 24 hours apart.

"Papi" broke Boston's single-season home run mark when he clouted 54 in 2006, surpassing Jimmie Foxx's record of 50. In five seasons with the Red Sox, Ortiz had amassed a .302 average with 208 homers and 642 RBI in 737 games.

# BOSTON'S FALL CLASSICS

BOSTON BABY BOOMERS remember where they were when JFK was shot, when Neil Armstrong set foot on the moon, and when the Berlin Wall came tumbling down. They also remember where they were when Carlton Fisk hit the walk-off homer in Game 6 of the 1975 World Series at 12:34 A.M. or when Mookie Wilson's roller trickled through Bill Buckner's legs late in Game 6 of the 1986 World Series. These, as well as other World Series moments, are forever embedded in the minds of Red Sox fans.

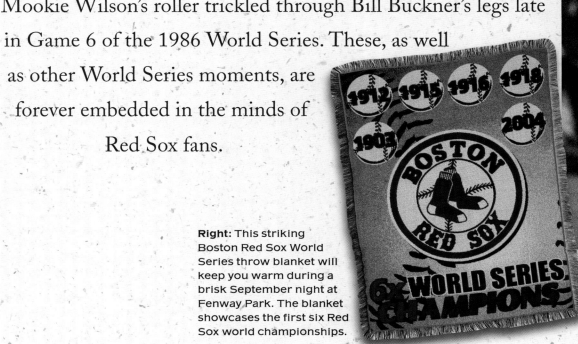

**Right:** This striking Boston Red Sox World Series throw blanket will keep you warm during a brisk September night at Fenway Park. The blanket showcases the first six Red Sox world championships.

**Above:** Bill Buckner is downcast after committing his infamous error in the 1986 World Series.
**Opposite Page:** Carlton Fisk smacked his legendary home run in the 1975 World Series.

# 1903

THE BOSTON AMERICANS were the toast of the town in 1903. They stood Boston on its head by playing in and winning the first World Series in history against the Pittsburgh Pirates.

The Americans drew phenomenal support at the Huntington Avenue Grounds, especially from a group of hardcore fans known as the "Royal Rooters." This group had a brass band, which played the theme song "Tessie" over and over during the eight games of the best-of-nine series. The crowds at Huntington were so overflowing that some of them stood in fair territory during the games.

Cy Young, Bill Dinneen, and Long Tom Hughes, all 20-game winners, led a strong Americans pitching staff. These hurlers were too much for a Pirates team that boasted Hall of Famer Honus Wagner, who was held to only six hits and committed six errors. Dinneen, who later became one of the great umpires of all time, struck out Wagner for the final out of the clinching game. The appreciative Boston crowd then swarmed manager Jimmy Collins's nine.

SOUVENIR CARD 10 CENTS

1903

McGREEVY

On the Avenue

Nuff said . . . .

3rd Base

..SOUVENIR CARD..

OF THE

World's Championship Games

Boston vs. Pittsburg

AMERICAN LEAGUE
BOSTON RED SOX
vs.
PITTSBURGH PIRATES
1st WORLD SERIES
OCT. 1 - 1903

**BOSTON A.L. (5) vs. PITTSBURGH N.L. (3)**

| | | | |
|---|---|---|---|
| Game 1 | Pittsburgh (Phillippe) | 7 | BOSTON (Young) 3 |
| Game 2 | BOSTON (Dinneen) | 3 | Pittsburgh (Leever) 0 |
| Game 3 | Pittsburgh (Phillippe) | 4 | BOSTON (Hughes) 2 |
| Game 4 | PITTSBURGH (Phillippe) | 5 | Boston (Dinneen) 4 |
| Game 5 | Boston (Young) | 11 | PITTSBURGH (Kennedy) 2 |
| Game 6 | Boston (Dinneen) | 6 | PITTSBURGH (Leever) 3 |
| Game 7 | Boston (Young) | 7 | PITTSBURGH (Phillippe) 3 |
| Game 8 | BOSTON (Dinneen) | 3 | Pittsburgh (Phillippe) 0 |

Managers—Jimmy Collins, Red Sox; Fred Clarke, Pirates

**Left and Above:** A 1903 souvenir card for the eighth game of baseball's first World Series. Boston won this game en route to becoming baseball's championship team. Imagine paying 10 cents for a souvenir card today?

**Far Left:** This poster features the players of the Boston Americans and their participation in the 1903 World Series. The poster, created years later, uses the franchise's present team name: "Red Sox."

This Official Score Card of the 1912 World Series depicts a New York Giant showing off his team's awesome record to a Red Sox player, who is dressed in Colonial clothes. In reality, the Giants failed to intimidate the Red Sox.

**BOSTON A.L. (4) vs. NEW YORK N.L. (3) 1 tie**

| | | | | |
|---|---|---|---|---|
| Game 1 | Boston (Wood) | 4 | NEW YORK (Tesreau) | 3 |
| Game 2 | BOSTON (tie) | *6 | New York (tie) | 6 |
| Game 3 | New York (Marquard) | 2 | BOSTON (O'Brien) | 1 |
| Game 4 | Boston (Wood) | 3 | NEW YORK (Tesreau) | 1 |
| Game 5 | BOSTON (Bedient) | 2 | New York (Mathewson) | 1 |
| Game 6 | NEW YORK (Marquard) | 5 | Boston (O'Brien) | 2 |
| Game 7 | New York (Tesreau) | 11 | BOSTON (Wood) | 4 |
| Game 8 | BOSTON (Wood) | **3 | New York (Mathewson) | 2 |

*11 innings                    **10 innings

Managers—Chick Stahl, Red Sox; John McGraw, Giants

# 1912

**A**S IT TURNS OUT, Bill Buckner's Game 6 gaffe in 1986 was merely the baseball gods' way of evening things out for what occurred in the 1912 World Series. In the eighth and deciding game of that World Series (a makeup game for Game 2, which had ended in a tie), Christy Mathewson of the New York Giants battled sore-armed Red Sox righty Smoky Joe Wood, who entered the game to relieve starting pitcher Hugh Bedient.

After the Giants took a 2–1 lead in the 10th, Giants center fielder Fred Snodgrass dropped Red Sox pinch-hitter Clyde Engle's routine fly ball with New York three outs away from winning the series. Engle took second base on the Snodgrass error, which became known as the "$30,000 Muff"—the difference between the winning and the losing share. Steve Yerkes walked, and Engle scored on Tris Speaker's single after the Giants gave Speaker a second chance by failing to catch a pop foul. The Red Sox eventually won on Larry Gardner's sacrifice fly, which scored Yerkes with the winning run.

The Red Sox had rallied to win the game, 3–2, and the World Series against the renown Christy Mathewson in what many consider the greatest World Series of the dead ball era.

Smoky Joe Wood was the hero of the 1912 World Series. He won three games for Boston, including the last one in relief.

# THE YEAR IT DIDN'T HAPPEN

If THE 1904 BOSTON AMERICANS could have anticipated an 86-year World Series drought for the franchise after 1918, they might have put up more of a fuss concerning the cancellation of the 1904 World Series. After beating the Pittsburgh Pirates in the 1903 World Series, they might have won back-to-back baseball championships.

The consensus, however, was that the National League champion New York Giants, with a dominant 106–47 record, would have trounced the Americans in the World Series. But we'll never know, because Giants owner John T. Brush took his ball and went home.

**Above:** Although the 1904 World Series never happened, the Boston Americans could still boast that they were the 1904 champions of the American League.
**Left:** Nobody deserves their place in the Hall of Fame more than pitching icon Cy Young. This Cy Young "Cooperstown" action figure shows the pitching great in his Boston Americans uniform.

The World Series had not become etched in stone as an annual event at that time, but the cancellation had nothing to do with that. Giants manager John McGraw had a running feud with American League President Ban Johnson after Johnson had suspended McGraw when he managed the American League Baltimore Orioles. And the Giants, who were confident that they would become the National League champions, did not want to risk losing against the junior circuit in a postseason playoff, especially to the crosstown upstart New York Highlanders (who nevertheless lost the AL pennant on the final day of the season to Boston and who, by the way, became the Yankees). For these two reasons, the Giants declared at midseason that they would not play in the World Series.

There were no rules in place to say they had to. To that point the World Series had just been an agreement between the winners of the two leagues, and Brush said no.

Too bad, because the 1904 Americans had some momentum. They had a veteran team with the likes of Buck Freeman, Freddy Parent, Chick Stahl, player-manager Jimmy Collins, and Candy LaChance, a group of ironmen who played virtually every day. They used only five pitchers the entire season with three 20-plus game winners in Cy Young, Bill Dinneen, and Jesse Tannehill.

The Americans produced a thrilling season in which they went 95–59, clinching the pennant in the first game of a doubleheader on the final day of the season against the New York Highlanders. In that game, Highlanders 41-game winner Jack Chesbro, on a two-strike count to Parent, threw a wild pitch that scored Lou Criger with the go-ahead run for Boston in the ninth inning.

The one good thing that happened as a result of no World Series is the backlash from fans, sports media, and baseball people. Guess who led the charge to make the World Series permanent? Giants owner John T. Brush. The following year, Brush's Giants beat the Philadelphia A's in the 1905 World Series while the Americans faded from view for a while.

Jimmy Collins was a defensive infielder extraordinaire who led Boston to victory in the first World Series in 1903. Collins was also a dependable clutch hitter who doubled as Boston's manager for several years. He was especially instrumental in leading the Boston Americans to the American League pennant in 1904.

# 1915

THE 1915 RED SOX won 101 regular-season games and gained a swagger that extended into the World Series, where they took care of the Philadelphia Phillies in five games.

Playing their home games at Braves Field in Boston to accommodate larger crowds, the Red Sox were so good that they didn't have to use 20-year-old lefty Babe Ruth, who had won 18 games during the regular season, or sore-armed Smoky Joe Wood in the World Series. In fact, their top three pitchers that year were Dutch Leonard, Ernie Shore, and Rube Foster. They outdueled a Philadelphia staff led by Grover Cleveland Alexander, who had gone 31–10 with a 1.22 ERA. Alexander beat the Red Sox in Game 1, 3–1, but that was as good as it got for the Phillies. Red Sox pitchers held the Phillies to a .182 average for the five games.

In an era of far fewer home runs, Red Sox right fielder Harry Hooper belted two of them, including the game-winner in a 5–4 Game 5 victory. Left fielder Duffy Lewis, who also starred in the series, homered in the same game. Boston enjoyed great defense from center fielder Tris Speaker and second baseman Jack Barry, who had been purchased from the Philadelphia A's on July 2 of that season, to go along with the pitching and the long ball.

**Above:** Harry Hooper's ninth inning home run in Game 5 of the 1915 World Series clinched another championship for Boston. The Red Sox defeated the Philadelphia Phillies four games to one in the fall classic.
**Right:** President Woodrow Wilson was the first president to attend a World Series game. No doubt, he was presented with this Souvenir Score Book for free.

Souvenir
SCORE BOOK
Price Ten Cents

RED SOX vs PHILADELPHIA
AMERICAN LEAGUE     NATIONAL LEAGUE

1915
WORLD'S SERIES
BRAVES FIELD · BOSTON, MASS.

1915

**BOSTON A.L. (4) vs. PHILADELPHIA N.L. (1)**

| | | | | |
|---|---|---|---|---|
| Game 1 | PHILADELPHIA (Alexander) | 3 | Boston (Shore) | 1 |
| Game 2 | Boston (Foster) | 2 | PHILADELPHIA (Mayer) | 1 |
| Game 3 | BOSTON (Leonard) | 2 | Philadelphia (Alexander) | 1 |
| Game 4 | BOSTON (Shore) | 2 | Philadelphia (Chalmers) | 1 |
| Game 5 | Boston (Foster) | 5 | PHILADELPHIA (Rixey) | 4 |

**Managers**—Bill Carrigan, Red Sox; Pat Moran, Phillies

# 1916

I'T'S RARE THAT you would name a manager as the main factor in a World Series championship. But Bill Carrigan, arguably the most successful Red Sox manager in history, did all the right things in his 1916 campaign as the Red Sox skipper.

They had lost the great Tris Speaker, who balked at having his pay cut and was traded to the Indians prior to the start of the season. Also, Smoky Joe Wood sat out the entire season with a sore arm. Through all of this, Carrigan motivated his players to overcome the absence of these two star players.

Babe Ruth won 23 games in 1916 with a 1.75 ERA and pitched brilliantly in a 2–1 win in 14 innings in Game 2; Del Gainer knocked in Mike McNally for the winning run. Twice in the Series the Red Sox peppered future Brooklyn Hall of Famer Rube Marquard. Conversely, Red Sox righty Ernie Shore won two big games, including the fifth and final game at Braves Field on October 12 as the Red Sox captured back-to-back World Series championships.

Carrigan was only 33 years old when he walked away from the game having won back-to-back titles. He returned to manage the Red Sox from 1927 through 1929, finishing dead last all three seasons.

**Top:** Many Red Sox fans pride themselves on collecting the most rare pieces of merchandise and memorabilia they can find, such as this 1916 iron-on patch.
**Above:** In Game 2 of the 1916 World Series, Hy Myers of the Brooklyn Robins (later the Dodgers) hit an inside-the-park home run in the first inning against Babe Ruth. It would be Brooklyn's only run of the game as Boston went on to win 2–1 in 14 innings.
**Left:** The 1916 Score Book did not look much different from the Score Book of the previous year. Only the name of the Red Sox opponent and a couple of faces changed.

## BOSTON A.L. (4) vs. BROOKLYN N.L. (1)

| | | | | |
|---|---|---|---|---|
| Game 1 | BOSTON (Shore) | 6 | Brooklyn (Marquard) | 5 |
| Game 2 | BOSTON (Ruth) | *2 | Brooklyn (Smith) | 1 |
| Game 3 | BROOKLYN (Coombs) | 4 | Boston (Mays) | 3 |
| Game 4 | Boston (Leonard) | 6 | BROOKLYN (Marquard) | 2 |
| Game 5 | BOSTON (Shore) | 4 | Brooklyn (Pfeiffer) | 1 |

*14 innings

Managers—Bill Carrigan, Red Sox; Wilbert Robinson, Dodgers

# 1918

GEORGE WHITEMAN was a relatively obscure player who had kicked around the minors for years, but he got his 15 minutes of fame in the 1918 World Series. The 35-year-old left fielder, who spent parts of three seasons in the major leagues, produced big hits and great catches in aiding Boston to a World Series victory over the Chicago Cubs in six games.

The relevance of 1918 cannot be overstated because it was the bookend of an 86-year championship drought for the Red Sox. World War I cut the regular season short, and the World Series was played in early September.

Babe Ruth pitched a 1–0 six-hit shutout in Game 1, and Carl Mays won two games including Game 6, the clincher. Whiteman, who made three great catches in Ruth's shutout, got his chance to play because Cubs manager Fred Mitchell started all left-handed pitchers in an effort to neutralize Ruth. Mitchell's strategy kept Ruth on the bench—except when he pitched—and out of the batter's box. But he couldn't account for Whiteman seizing the moment and forging his legacy.

Whiteman, who was all of 5'7", hit only .250 for the series, but *Sport Magazine* writer F. C. Lane wrote: "Several times during the series it devolved around Whiteman to save the game for the Red Sox. And every time he rose to the occasion." In the eighth inning of Game 6, Whiteman, who had a hand in driving in both runs in Boston's 2–1 deciding win, made what Lane described as "one of the most sensational stops ever made on the diamond"— a shoestring somersaulting catch—to end a potential Cubs rally, which essentially secured a World Series victory in six games.

The game was nearly not played because players were threatening to strike unless they received a larger percentage of the ticket revenues. Even though baseball executives were shortchanging them on their winnings, the players reluctantly agreed to take the field but only in tribute to the soldiers who were fighting in World War I.

With the 1918 World Series, Whiteman's career ended in glory. He never played again.

BOSTON A.L. (4) vs. CHICAGO N.L. (2)

| Game 1 | Boston (Ruth) | 1 | CHICAGO (Vaughn) | 0 |
| Game 2 | CHICAGO (Tyler) | 3 | Boston (Bush) | 1 |
| Game 3 | Boston (Mays) | 2 | CHICAGO (Vaughn) | 1 |
| Game 4 | BOSTON (Ruth) | 3 | Chicago (Douglas) | 2 |
| Game 5 | Chicago (Vaughn) | 3 | BOSTON (Jones) | 0 |
| Game 6 | BOSTON (Mays) | 2 | Chicago (Tyler) | 1 |

Managers—Ed Barrow, Red Sox; Fred Mitchell, Cubs

The cover of this 1918 Score Card is more about cigarette, chewing gum, cigar, and tire ads than about baseball. This blatant commercialism is unique among World Series Score Cards and later World Series programs.

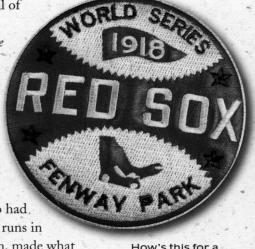

How's this for a unique piece of Red Sox memorabilia? It is a Red Sox iron-on patch from one of the most amazing years in team history: 1918.

Fred Merkle of the Chicago Cubs takes a lead off first base while Carl Mays of the Boston Red Sox stands on the pitcher's mound. Ten years earlier, Merkle had made a bonehead mistake that cost the New York Giants the 1908 pennant. The beneficiary of his mistake was the Chicago Cubs, who went on to win their last World Series. Carl Mays won this game in the 1918 World Series, which was the last World Series that the Red Sox won until 2004.

# THE CURSE OF THE BAMBINO

THE 2004 BOSTON RED SOX not only brought a World Series to Boston for the first time in 86 years, but they lifted the storied "Curse of the Bambino" from the shoulders of Red Sox Nation. The Curse of the Bambino began with the notorious sale of baseball's greatest player, George Herman "Babe" Ruth, to the hated New York Yankees.

In 1919, then-Red Sox owner Harry Frazee sold "The Babe" to the team's bitter rivals, some claim, to fund his Broadway musical, *No, No, Nanette*. The sale was considered a ridiculous and shocking move at the time, but no one could have anticipated the effect Frazee's transaction would have on Red Sox Nation for years to come. It should be noted, however, that Ruth was driving management and his teammates up the wall with his off-the-field antics and that he was holding out for more money. Also, the other teams either wouldn't or couldn't afford to trade with the Red Sox.

**Above:** Seen here are two of baseball's biggest superstars, Lou Gehrig (left) and Babe Ruth. When the Bambino was not slugging his way into the history books for the Yankees, he took some time out to play the sax (much to Gehrig's dismay).
**Left:** Two famous songs—"Tea for Two" and "I Want to Be Happy"—came from this English musical comedy. This Broadway production opened on September 16, 1925, five years after Frazee sold Ruth, and ran for 321 performances.

In any case, every bad call, every bounce through a fielder's legs, and every late-inning home run by less-than-formidable opposing hitters seemed astoundingly woven together as a consequence of the Curse. And each incident was more excruciating than the last.

After Bucky Dent homered over the Green Monster in the seventh inning of the 1978 one-game playoff between the Red Sox and Yankees, costing the Red Sox their season, the Curse would be blamed. After New York Met Mookie Wilson's grounder bounced through Bill Buckner's legs in Game 6 of the 1986 World Series, the Curse would again be blamed. After manager Grady Little inexplicably left a tired Pedro Martinez in the game during the eighth inning of Game 7 of the 2003 ALCS, the Curse would be blamed once more for the Red Sox loss.

The Red Sox had won five of the first 15 World Series ever played, while the lowly Yankees never won any. Coincidentally or not, however, the tide changed dramatically for future generations. The Yankees went on to win 26 World Series. The Red Sox went to four World Series after the sale of Ruth and lost all four … each in Game 7.

When Theo Epstein took the reins of the Red Sox as general manager in 2003, he vowed that Red Sox luck would change. He built a devastating offense and a dominant rotation. Finally, the 2004 Red Sox made a name for themselves when they became the only team in baseball history to come back from a 3–0 deficit to win the ALCS against the Yankees. Next, they lifted the Curse of the Bambino from their shoulders in their four-game World Series sweep of the St. Louis Cardinals.

These two coins commemorate Babe Ruth's legendary stint with the New York Yankees. His number 3, of course, has been retired.

# 1946

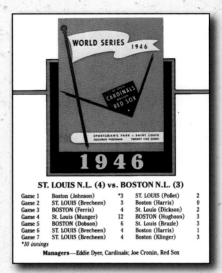

**T**EAMMATES ABSOLVED Johnny Pesky of all blame for Enos Slaughter's "mad dash" from first to home in Game 7 of the 1946 World Series, which led to Boston's defeat at the hands of the St. Louis Cardinals. "Nobody on our team ever, ever blamed Johnny," said Dominic DiMaggio, who had to come out of Game 7 after a double in the eighth. He pulled up lame, forcing manager Joe Cronin to install Leon Culberson in center in the bottom of the eighth.

| | WORLD SERIES 1946 |
| --- | --- |

**ST. LOUIS N.L. (4) vs. BOSTON N.L. (3)**

| | | |
| --- | --- | --- |
| Game 1 | Boston (Johnson) *3 | ST. LOUIS (Pollet) 2 |
| Game 2 | ST. LOUIS (Brecheen) 3 | Boston (Harris) 0 |
| Game 3 | BOSTON (Ferris) 4 | St. Louis (Dickson) 2 |
| Game 4 | St. Louis (Munger) 12 | BOSTON (Hughson) 3 |
| Game 5 | BOSTON (Dobson) 6 | St. Louis (Brazle) 3 |
| Game 6 | ST. LOUIS (Brecheen) 4 | Boston (Harris) 1 |
| Game 7 | ST. LOUIS (Brecheen) 4 | Boston (Klinger) 3 |

*10 innings
**Managers**—Eddie Dyer, Cardinals; Joe Cronin, Red Sox

Pesky was severely criticized for hesitating before throwing home, but numerous replays show that Culberson made a weak cutoff throw to Pesky. The Red Sox shortstop had to wheel and fire to the plate and had no chance at the speedy Slaughter.

Despite Ted Williams's elbow injury and despite Bobby Doerr and DiMaggio both being banged up, the Red Sox came just one game short of winning it all. Much like John McNamara in 1986 and Darrell Johnson in 1975, Cronin was criticized for poor management of his personnel, but Cronin actually did a great job of holding this team together.

**Above:** The cover of this Souvenir Program shows that the Cardinal home games were played at Sportsman's Park, which would later be called Busch Stadium.
**Far Left:** The 1946 Boston Red Sox yearbook is a rare collector's item. The Red Sox finished 97–57 and reached the World Series for the first time in the Tom Yawkey era.
**Left:** Rudy York got the Red Sox off to a fast start in the 1946 World Series, winning Game 1 with a home run in the tenth inning. Bobby Doerr greets York at home plate.

# 1967

CONSIDER THAT St. Louis Cardinals ace Bob Gibson won three games, pitched 27 innings, and struck out 26 with five walks and a 1.00 ERA. Still, a Red Sox staff led by Jim Lonborg, who pitched an impressive one-hit shutout in Game 2, held the Cards to a .223 average while future Hall of Famer Orlando Cepeda was limited to a .103 (3-for-29) average.

The Cardiac Kids were young and brash, and the Cardinals experienced and savvy. Some believe the only thing that stood between winning the series and losing, as Boston did in seven games, was being unable to match Lonborg up against Gibson for Games 1, 4, and 7 because they didn't clinch the American League pennant until the last day of the regular season.

Despite Gibson's dominance, the Red Sox refused to back down. Lonborg threw a fastball under Lou Brock's chin to lead off Game 2, which set the tone for the remainder of the series. They even beat a young Cardinal lefty named Steve Carlton.

"When it was over we were disappointed, but we knew what we had accomplished," said the late Eddie Popowski, the team's third base coach.

Carl Yastrzemski watches a ball sail over the scoreboard in left field at Fenway Park. Julian Javier's three-run homer off Jim Lonborg in the top of the sixth pretty much assured the Cards of winning Game 7 of the 1967 World Series. The final score was 7–2.

# YOUNG TRAGEDIES

**T**WO OF THE GREATEST athletes in New England history—Tony Conigliaro and Harry Agganis—had their careers and lives end tragically, leaving Red Sox fans to wonder what might have been.

Conigliaro was 19, a year removed from St. Marys High School in 1964, when he made his Red Sox debut. At age 22, he became the youngest major-leaguer to hit his 100th homer. But on August 18, 1967, a Jack Hamilton fastball beaned him in the left eye, and despite two comeback attempts, his career ended in 1975.

"We were looking at 600 homers if he had a full career," recalled Conigliaro's manager, Johnny Pesky. "He would have been a Hall of Famer." Conigliaro, who was a fitness buff and had become a TV reporter in San Francisco, suffered a heart attack and lapsed into a coma in January 1982 while his brother Billy was driving him to a Boston TV interview. He spent the last eight years of his life as an invalid before passing on at age 45.

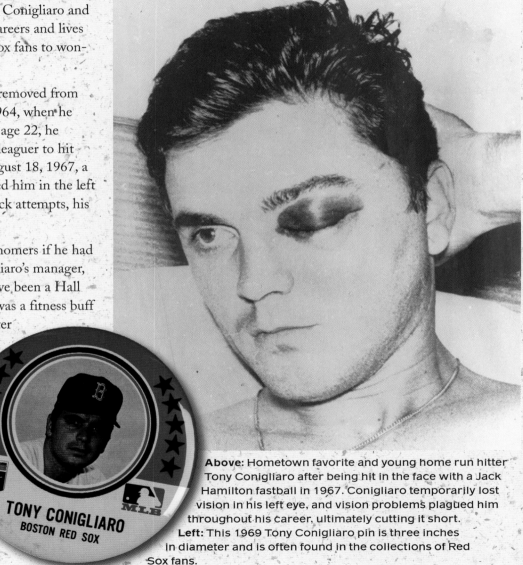

**Above:** Hometown favorite and young home run hitter Tony Conigliaro after being hit in the face with a Jack Hamilton fastball in 1967. Conigliaro temporarily lost vision in his left eye, and vision problems plagued him throughout his career, ultimately cutting it short.
**Left:** This 1969 Tony Conigliaro pin is three inches in diameter and is often found in the collections of Red Sox fans.

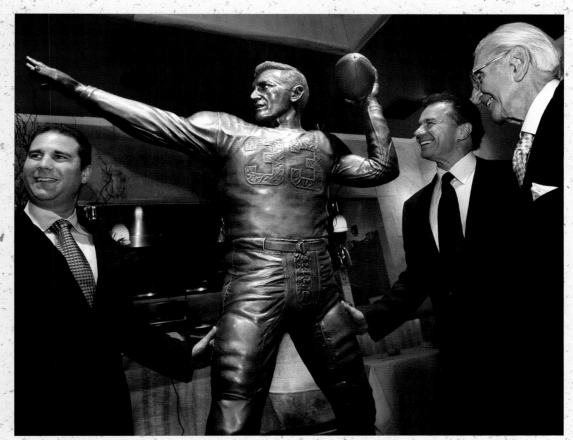

This life-size bronze statue of Harry Agganis is unveiled at the Meze restaurant in Boston's Charlestown on May 4, 2004. Armand LaMontagne was the sculptor. Agganis himself was a two-sport athlete who played first base for the Red Sox in 1954 and 1955. He died tragically at 26 of a pulmonary embolism. Boston University named its indoor sports complex after Agganis, who was a phenomenal quarterback for BU.

Agganis was considered the greatest all-around athlete ever to come out of New England. A graduate of Lynn Classical High and Boston University, he turned down $50,000 from the NFL's Cleveland Browns to play for the Red Sox. After one year at Triple-A Louisville, Agganis played in 1954 and part of 1955. The lefty first base-man hit a disappointing .251 with 11 homers as a rookie, but he vowed to be a .300 hitter. By the second week in May 1955, he was hitting .313.

Agganis was stricken with viral pneumonia. He tried to come back too soon. He relapsed and also incurred phlebitis. As late June approached, Agganis was feeling better, but suddenly and without warning, he passed away when he suffered a massive pulmonary embolism. Agganis's funeral drew a crowd of more than 20,000 to St. George's Greek Orthodox Church in Lynn. The funeral was one of the largest outlays of grieving ever witnessed in that town.

Pesky sadly commented on these two Boston players whose promise of greatness was unlimited but never fulfilled: "Agganis was special. Baseball wasn't even his best sport. Tony was a great hitter and outfielder. A superstar in the making."

# 1975

THERE WERE MORE twists and turns in the 1975 World Series than in Luis Tiant's distorted delivery. Most of them were centered around Game 6 when Carlton Fisk shocked the world with a 12th-inning walk-off homer to force a Game 7.

Even prior to that, however, Bernie Carbo's incredible three-run game-tying homer in the bottom of the eighth inning of Game 6 saved the Series. There was also Dwight Evans's stunning backhanded catch of Joe Morgan's home run bid near the bullpen in right field in the 11th, which served as Fisk's chance to do the unimaginable.

"That was baseball," recalled Pete Rose many years later. "That Series is what you play for."

Luis Tiant won Game 1 6–0, bedazzling the Big Red Machine lineup. It is not an exaggeration to say he whet the appetite of an entire nation, a majority of which had believed the Reds would romp.

After the Red Sox lost Game 2 3–2, the series shifted to Cincinnati. Carbo and Dwight Evans each hit two-run homers to erase a 5–1 Reds lead in Game 3, but in the bottom of the 10th home plate umpire Larry

**CINCINNATI N.L. (4) vs. BOSTON A.L. (3)**

| Game 1 | BOSTON (Tiant) | 6 | Cincinnati (Gullett) | 0 |
| Game 2 | Cincinnati (Eastwick) | 3 | BOSTON (Drago) | 2 |
| Game 3 | CINCINNATI (Eastwick) | *6 | Boston (Willoughby) | 5 |
| Game 4 | Boston (Tiant) | 5 | CINCINNATI (Norman) | 4 |
| Game 5 | CINCINNATI (Gullett) | 6 | Boston (Cleveland) | 2 |
| Game 6 | BOSTON (Wise) | **7 | Cincinnati (Darcy) | 6 |
| Game 7 | Cincinnati (Carroll) | 4 | BOSTON (Burton) | 3 |
| *10 innings | **12 innings | | (Night Games: Games 3-7) | |

Managers—Sparky Anderson, Reds; Darrell Johnson, Red Sox

**Left:** Red Sox second baseman Denny Doyle pivots as he starts a double play before the crowd at Fenway.
**Far Left:** The cover to this 1975 program features a beautiful collage of baseball players in action.
**Below:** Like many World Series team pennants, this 1975 Red Sox souvenir lists Boston's roster. Boston faithful who own this pennant recall the faces that go with each name.

WORLD SERIES · *Boston* RED SOX 1975 · AMERICAN LEAGUE CHAMPIONS

RICE · CARBO · EVANS · BURTON · MORET · POLE · SEGUI · DRAGO · LEE · MILLER · TIANT · FISK · MONTGOMERY · BENIQUEZ · PETROCELLI · WISE · LYNN · COOPER · WILLOUGHBY · BLACKWELL · BURLESON · CLEVELAND · YASTRZEMSKI · GRIFFIN · DOYLE · HEISE

MGR. JOHNSON

Barnett missed an important call. Replays on TV screens across America showed clearly that Ed Armbrister interfered with Fisk on a sacrifice bunt that bounced straight up in the air at home plate. As Fisk fielded the ball and attempted to throw to second, Armbrister blocked Fisk, who threw the ball errantly into center field. The Reds went on to rally and won the game on Morgan's single.

Tiant evened the Series when he won Game 4 to erase what momentum the Reds had built up. The Reds came back in Game 5 behind Don Gullett's pitching and Tony Perez's homer. Then in Game 6, the Red Sox again evened the series by edging the Reds in extra innings.

For almost six innings, the Red Sox were in command of Game 7 behind Bill Lee, leading 3–0 before it fell apart for them. Jim Willoughby had been pitching lights-out in relief, but in the eighth, manager Darrell Johnson yanked him for a pinch-hitter. Johnson stunned all by going with young lefty Jim Burton, who surrendered the go-ahead and ultimately Series-winning hit to Morgan, ending the Series for the Reds.

Catcher Johnny Bench of the Cincinnati Reds holds onto the ball after Fred Lynn slides across home plate during the 1975 World Series at Fenway.

# 1986

Dennis "Oil Can" Boyd never got to pitch Game 7. Dave Stapleton never replaced Bill Buckner for defense late in Game 6. Dave "Hendu" Henderson, the best player Boston had in the 1986 postseason, had run out of miracle hits.

Oh yes, this series has stuck in the craw of most Red Sox fans. While there were 86 long years between championships, the wait between 1986 and 2004 was even more insufferable. Despite the sadness and disappointment, this team defied the odds and finished first in the AL East for the first time in 11 years.

In the playoffs against the California Angels, Hendu brought them back from a three-games-to-one deficit and one strike away from elimination. They went on to easily win Games 6 and 7 of the AL Championship Series.

The Red Sox were one strike away from finally winning the World Series before Bob Stanley's wild pitch/Rich Gedman's passed ball (pick your poison) and the ultimate indignity—a routine grounder going through Bill Buckner's legs in the bottom of the 10th of Game 6. There was that sickening scene of champagne bottles being wheeled out of the Red Sox locker room, and the large sheets of plastic that had been put up to protect the lockers from champagne spray were torn down.

Calvin Schiraldi entered Game 6 of the 1986 World Series in the eighth inning with a 3–2 lead. No one could have anticipated what followed. He became the losing pitcher of both Game 6 and Game 7. Although he finished the 1986 regular season with a 1.41 ERA, he was never the same reliever after the 1986 postseason.

"It was bouncing, bouncing, bouncing . . . then it went under," Buckner told the press after the game. "I haven't missed a ground ball in two months. What a hell of a one to miss. I played it a lot deeper than normal. It was a hit that had a lot of spin."

The Red Sox also had Game 7 in the bag, but they squandered a 3–0 lead in the sixth inning when starter Bruce Hurst lost his command. The Mets rallied as Ray Knight hit a tie-breaking homer against Calvin Schiraldi, and soon it was over.

It was an unusual series from the outset as the Red Sox won the first two games at Shea Stadium, and then lost two out of three at Fenway. But they had a 3–2 lead going back to Shea and had leads in Games 6 and 7—only to squander them.

**Right:** Dennis "Oil Can" Boyd pitches from the Fenway Park mound. Known for his colorful personality, "Oil Can" was an important contributor to Boston's 1986 American League championship season.
**Far Right:** This classy 1986 World Series Program sold for $5, quite a jump from 10 cents in 1903.

OFFICIAL 1986 WORLD SERIES PROGRAM $5.00

# WILLIAMS vs. FRANCONA

1967 WORLD SERIES - 30TH ANNIVERSARY

BOSTON, MA
OCT
12
1997
02205

*Dick Williams*

APPEARING IN THEIR FIRST WORLD SERIES IN 21 YEARS, THE BOSTON RED SOX HOSTED THE ST. LOUIS CARDINALS FOR GAME 1. SERIES MVP BOB GIBSON BEAT THE SOX 2-1, BUT JIM LONBORG EVENED THE SERIES WITH A 5-0 WIN IN GAME 2 AS CARL YASTRZEMSKI HOMERED TWICE. THE CARDINALS TOOK THE NEXT TWO GAMES, INCLUDING GIBSON'S SECOND WIN IN GAME 4. BOSTON EVENED THE SERIES WITH WINS IN GAME 5 AND 6, HIGHLIGHTED BY YASTRZEMSKI AND RICO PETROCELLI HOME RUNS. HOWEVER, GIBSON WON 7-2 IN GAME 7 FOR HIS THIRD SERIES WIN, LEADING THE CARDINALS TO THE TITLE.

BOSTON RED SOX
VS.
ST. LOUIS CARDINALS

**D**ICK WILLIAMS and Terry Francona were first-year managers who directed two of the most important teams in recent Red Sox history. Williams managed the "Impossible Dream" Red Sox, and Francona managed the team that pulled off the first World Series win since 1918 with 2004's band of self-proclaimed "idiots."

The irony here? Francona played for Dick Williams in Montreal in 1981, Francona's rookie season. So whose job was tougher?

Williams was tough on young players, which is why his management of the 1967 team was remarkably successful. Moreover, some of the young Red Sox players in 1967 had played for Williams at Triple-A Toronto. Williams took over a team that had finished ninth in the American League in 1966, and there was no pressure to do anything but improve. Carl Yastrzemski was the oldest player in Boston's starting lineup, and he was 27.

Francona had the unenviable task of managing a club with high expectations, especially one that lost Game 7 of the American

**Left:** Dick Williams pulled off one of the great managerial feats in sports history. He turned the morbid 1966 Red Sox season into the Impossible Dream season of 1967 with a style of hard-nose discipline that resonated with his players.
**Below Left:** This 1997 cover commemorates the 1967 World Series and bears the autograph of Boston manager Dick Williams. Notice that the envelope was stamped on October 12, which is the day—30 years earlier—that the seventh game of the World Series was played in Boston.

League Championship Series in 2003 to New York the previous year. Nothing less than taking the Red Sox to the World Series would be tolerated.

Still, although Francona had more proven talent than Williams, Williams had a few surprises. One was Yaz's winning the Triple Crown. The other was Jim Lonborg's 22 wins. Francona nearly had a superstar team with a star at virtually every position. His Lonborg was Curt Schilling, who won 21 games. Francona's Yaz was Big Papi, and Francona also had Manny Ramirez—certainly a future Hall of Famer.

Red Sox great Jim Rice was asked which manager he thought had the tougher job. Rice said, "I think Terry Francona. The reason is that it's a lot tougher to manage players in this era than it was back then. Now you have players making more money than the manager. The players of today aren't as mature as the players were back then. I think there was a lot more respect for the manager then. The manager now has so many issues he has to deal with. For me, for Terry to have got that group together and won a championship, that's saying a lot."

**Top:** This is an autographed Terry Francona baseball. Upon his arrival in Boston, "Tito" was met with a lot of skepticism about where he could lead the Red Sox. He quickly silenced the critics by winning the World Series in his first year with the club.
**Above:** Terry Francona on the first day of the toughest job he'll ever have: Boston Red Sox manager. Francona has handled the high-pressure position with dignity and class.

# 2004

THE 2004 WORLD SERIES didn't engender the drama and excitement of 1946, 1967, 1975, or 1986, but it didn't have to. The difference between 2004 and the other World Series was obvious—the Red Sox won it. Easily, in fact. A four-game sweep of the St. Louis Cardinals ended curses and realigned the baseball planets after 86 years of the Red Sox orbiting in oblivion.

De facto leader Johnny Damon recollected two years later, "We were not going to be denied after what we went through to beat the Yankees in the playoffs. I think a lot of people might have felt as though we left everything we had in that series. But we wanted to finish it off. We knew what we had to do."

The Red Sox had never dominated any team in the World Series like they did the St. Louis Cardinals, to whom they had lost the fall classic in 1946 and 1967.

After closer Keith Foulke fielded Cardinal Edgar Renteria's tapper back to the mound and underhanded a throw to first baseman Doug Mientkiewicz for the final out of Game 4, the players celebrated their feat—first on the old Busch Stadium field, which hosted its last World Series before demoli-

tion, and then in the cramped quarters of the visiting clubhouse. Past and present members of the Red Sox enjoyed their long overdue prize.

The Cardinals had won 105 games during the regular season, but the Red Sox pitching held the Cards to a .190 average, including a horrible 0-for-15 by cleanup hitter Scott Rolen. Manny Ramirez was named the World Series MVP with a .412 average.

"We learned a lot from the Yankee series," said Ramirez, who told teammates before Game 4, "Let's not let these guys breathe."

A Red Sox Nation could barely breathe when the Red Sox wound up winning eight straight postseason games to end their 86-year curse.

**Above:** This souvenir Red Sox license plate can be seen everywhere in Boston. It is a reminder of one of the most thrilling events in New England history.
**Opposite Page:** Red Sox closer Keith Foulke and first baseman Doug Mientkiewicz raise their arms in triumph after Edgar Renteria grounded out to end the 2004 World Series.

# MAGICAL RED SOX MOMENTS

Ted Williams awaits Bob Feller's pitch in a 1953 game against the Cleveland Indians at Municipal Stadium. Williams was a fighter pilot in the Korean War just a few months prior to this at-bat.

IN ALMOST EVERY decade of Red Sox lore, there was something that kept you on the edge of your seat. Whether it was Ted's many unbelievable feats from 1939 to 1960, Yaz's unforgettable "Impossible Dream" moments, Roger striking out 20 batters ten years apart, or Big Papi's walk-off homers.

**Opposite Page:** The Red Sox players celebrate their victory over the St. Louis Cardinals in the 2004 World Series. They swept their opponents in four games.
**Below:** This vintage Ted Williams pin is 1¼" in diameter. Some claim this souvenir is from the '40s; others say from the '50s. Can you tell from his picture?

# Cy Young's Triple Crown in 1901

**H**E HAD COME to Boston in 1901 amidst hype that would rival Pedro Martinez's Red Sox debut in 1997 or Daisuke Matsuzaka showing up at the Red Sox spring training camp in 2007. In 1901, the hoopla might have been a little quieter. Young, who had won 25 or more games for Cleveland every year from 1891 to 1898, went to St. Louis briefly but left after only two years because he felt he was underpaid, and he didn't care for that city's humidity and heat. He joined the Boston Americans in 1901 at age 34 when he jumped to the new league, becoming Boston's first superstar.

In his first season, Young won the Triple Crown for pitchers. He posted 33 wins (including five shutouts), a 1.62 ERA, and 158 strikeouts. In 371 innings, he walked only 37. During the course of the year, he passed the 300-win mark for his career.

Young pitched for Boston through 1908 before being dealt back to Cleveland. Meanwhile, he was the whole show and the talk of Beantown whenever he took the mound.

**Above Left:** You won't find too many old cloth baseball patches around. Here is one of Cy Young, the greatest pitcher of his era.
**Above:** Cy Young winds up in this rare shot from 1908. Boston played its home games at the Huntington Avenue Grounds until 1912. Today, Northeastern University's Solomon Court at Cabot Center sits atop the former Grounds.

Imagine if Manny Ramirez was a Cy Young candidate...or if Curt Schilling drove in more than 100 runs...Babe Ruth's greatness as both a pitcher and a hitter makes the argument that he's the best ever almost indisputable.

# On July 21, 1915, Babe Ruth Did It All

AMAZINGLY, this date is a mere footnote in Babe Ruth's magnificent career. He was only 20 and starting to yearn to be a full-time hitter rather than a pitcher. In fact, Ruth showed he could do it all.

The young Babe went 4-for-4 with a single, two doubles, and a tape-measure homer that cleared Sportsman's Park in St. Louis, home of the St. Louis Browns. The home run was one of the longest ever seen at the ballpark, sailing outside the stadium and onto Grand Avenue. Ruth was also the starting pitcher that day, recording a 4–2 win.

That year, the Red Sox already had one of the most talented outfields in Red Sox history, with Tris Speaker in center, Duffy Lewis in left, and Harry Hooper in right. But even as the pitcher, Ruth hit .315 in 92 at-bats with four homers (the first four of his career) and 21 RBI. He went 18–8 with a 2.44 ERA.

# Ted Williams's 1941 All-Star Game Heroics

**T**ED WILLIAMS ONCE called it "the most thrilling hit of my life." Quite a statement considering his body of work, especially in 1941 when he became the last player to hit .400 (.406).

The 22-year-old Williams, hitting .405 at the time, never thought he'd be allowed to bat in the bottom of the ninth in the 1941 All-Star Game, not only because he was scheduled to be the sixth hitter but also because he never thought the National League would pitch to him. The score was 5–3 when the American Leaguers came to bat. Then, after Joe DiMaggio ran hard to beat out what should have been a double-play grounder, Williams came up with two on and two out for the American League.

Dom DiMaggio, who was on deck, figured "they were going to put Ted on and pitch to me." Didn't happen. On a 2–1 slider thrown by Cubs right-hander Claude Passeau, Williams launched a game-winning three-run bomb off the right-field roof at Briggs Stadium in Detroit, turning a 5–4 deficit into a 7–5 win. The crowd went wild. Williams jumped around the bases clapping with a youthful enthusiasm that's frozen in time.

**Above:** Ted Williams crosses home plate after his dramatic walk-off home run in the 1941 All-Star Game. Ted smiles ear to ear as his friend and rival Joe DiMaggio congratulates him.

**Left:** There's all kinds of merchandise available for Red Sox fans. If you're a true old-time fan, you can wear Teddy Ballgame's pin, denoting his six batting titles, to the next Red Sox game.

TED WILLIAMS
★ 6 ★
BATTING TITLES
1941 ✕ 1942
1947 ✕ 1948
1957 ✕ 1958
BOSTON
RED SOX

# Williams Ends Up at .406 on Final Day of 1941 Season

**T**ED WILLIAMS ENTERED the final day of the 1941 season at Philadelphia's Shibe Park with a .3995 batting average, which would have been rounded up to .400. Probably because he believed he was the "greatest hitter who ever lived," Williams had no intentions of sitting out the scheduled doubleheader against the Philadelphia A's.

Adding to the drama of the day was Lefty Grove's farewell performance in the second game of the twin bill. It was all the more reason for Williams to play—not to mention that the Boston press would have unloaded on their favorite punching bag.

While newspaper accounts indicated Williams was nervous heading into the final day, he ended that quickly, going 4-for-5 with a home run in the first game to raise his average to .404 in a 12–11 Red Sox win. In Grove's final game, Williams went 2-for-3 to finish the season with an astounding .406 average!

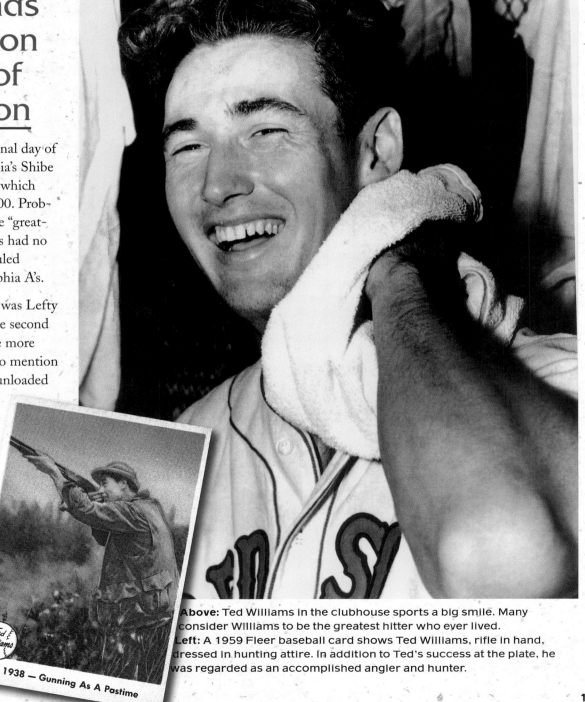

1938 — Gunning As A Pastime

**Above:** Ted Williams in the clubhouse sports a big smile. Many consider Williams to be the greatest hitter who ever lived.
**Left:** A 1959 Fleer baseball card shows Ted Williams, rifle in hand, dressed in hunting attire. In addition to Ted's success at the plate, he was regarded as an accomplished angler and hunter.

# TIMELESS MOON SHOTS

OFFICIALLY, THE HOME RUN recognized as the longest in Red Sox history was Ted Williams's 502-foot shot off Detroit right-hander Fred Hutchinson into the right field bleachers at Fenway on June 9, 1946. "He threw me a change-up, and I saw it coming," Williams told *The Boston Globe* some 50 years later. "I picked it up fast, and I just whaled into it." At the time, Williams's homer was measured at 450 feet; it was recalculated to 502 feet in 1984.

The ball knocked the straw hat off of Joe Boucher, a 56-year-old construction engineer from Albany, New York, who often attended Red Sox games when he was in town. Boucher was treated for injuries at Fenway's medical center and returned to watch the remainder of the game. "How far away must one sit to be safe in the park?" Boucher asked. "I didn't even get the ball. They say it bounced a dozen rows higher. But after it hit my head, I was no longer interested. I couldn't see the ball. The sun was right in our eyes. All we could do was duck."

Other clouts have also been much dis-

Mo Vaughn hits his second home run of the game against Baltimore in 1996. Vaughn hit .326 with 44 homers and 143 RBI that year.

cussed. Manny Ramirez struck a ball into the light tower in left field on June 23, 2001, against Toronto's Chris Michalak. The Red Sox public relations staff estimated that the ball traveled 501 feet. Ramirez hit another blast into the upper deck in Toronto's Sky-Dome. Mo Vaughn almost got one out of Baltimore's Memorial Stadium in right field. And Dwight Evans hit one halfway up the upper deck in left at Yankee Stadium.

Jim Rice once hit a ball that cleared the right side of Fenway's flag pole in left field. There was Jimmie Foxx's 1936 blast off Yankee righty Red Ruffing. It landed on the back roof of the Lansdowne Street parking garage on the fly. Foxx also cleared left field at Chicago's Comiskey Park during his Red Sox career.

On June 19, 1977, Carl Yastrzemski hit the right-field facade at Fenway in the eighth inning, 20 feet to the right of where No. 42 (in honor of Jackie Robinson) is currently retired. It is the only ball ever to reach that spot.

**Above:** Manny Ramirez clenches his fist as he rounds the bases after slugging a 491-foot home run into Toronto's fifth deck on June 3, 2001. Ramirez's blast eclipsed Mark McGwire's 1996 record 488-foot homer at the SkyDome.
**Left:** Ramirez was arguably the best active right-handed hitter of his era in baseball, and this autographed ball is a true collector's item.

# Sox Score 17 Runs in One Inning on June 18, 1953

WHILE THE GREAT Ted Williams was fighting in the Korean War, the Red Sox were still able to score 17 runs in the seventh inning of a 23–3 romp over the Detroit Tigers on June 18, 1953.

The Red Sox sent the batting order up four short of three times (23 batters), and the Tigers used three different pitchers to no avail. The Red Sox mustered 14 hits and six walks. Gene Stephens had three hits in the inning, which set a major-league record, and Dick Gernert drove in four of the 17 runs. What is even more remarkable is that the Tigers committed none of their five errors in this inning.

**Above:** This Red Sox pin displays two bats. Many times in their illustrious history, the Red Sox possessed a powerful offense, which was certainly evident on June 18, 1953.

**Right:** Jimmy Piersall played right field in this game. He stroked two hits and drove in three runs, two of which were in the seventh inning.

"It just seemed like everything was a base hit or a walk," Stephens told *The Boston Globe*'s Gordon Edes many years later. "There are two things I remember about the game. I remember the manager for Detroit—one of the greatest guys to ever put on a uniform, Fred Hutchinson—a big ol' burly guy. The other thing I remember, George Kell made two outs in the inning—one to end the inning—and both were line drives. Gosh, it's been so long ago. I got two singles and a double, but there wasn't much made of it at the time."

That's because only 3,108 fans were on hand at Fenway that day.

# Pumpsie Green Becomes the First African American to Play for the Red Sox on July 21, 1959

Jackie Robinson's daughter Sharon throws out the first pitch on the 50th anniversary of the start to her father's career during the Red Sox home opener at Fenway on April 11, 1997. Pumpsie Green, the first African-American to play for the Red Sox, is at her side.

NEARLY 38 YEARS after becoming the first African-American player to ever play for the Red Sox, Pumpsie Green remembered, "It was an emotional, nerve-wracking day."

While he had made his Red Sox debut on July 21 in Chicago as a pinch-runner, he got into his first Fenway game two weeks later playing second base. He helped turn a double-play, taking a grounder from third baseman Frank Malzone and then turning the twin-killing with a strong throw to first baseman Pete Runnels.

"I ran off the field and into the dugout and got a bat," he told *The Boston Globe*. "I walked up to the plate and got a standing ovation from the crowd. It was heartwarming. I got lucky and hit a triple off the left-center fence."

After Green befriended Ted Williams, he warmed up with Williams before every game between that day and Williams's last game on September 28, 1960.

# WHAT'S BETTER THAN A RED SOX ROUT?

THERE HAVE BEEN many Red Sox routs through the years, but none was bigger than the Red Sox's 29–4 bashing of the St. Louis Browns on June 8, 1950, before 5,105 fans at Fenway Park. In fact, it is the biggest rout in modern major-league history. The Red Sox pounded 28 hits—seven of them were homers and nine were doubles. Bobby Doerr smacked three home runs while Ted Williams and Walt Dropo both hit a pair. Leadoff batter Clyde Vollmer also set a major-league mark of his own as the only batter to go to the plate eight times in eight innings.

The day before, the Red Sox had crushed the hapless Browns 20–4. The old Browns were a team that the Red Sox just slapped silly. The year before they had clobbered them 21–2 on June 24.

A franchise that has traditionally had big boppers, the Red Sox have exercised their muscle often. A recent instance came on June 27, 2003, when the Red Sox humiliated the Florida Marlins at Fenway 25–8. The Marlins starting pitcher in that game was former Red Sox farmhand Carl Pavano, who pitched to six batters—all of whom came home. The Red Sox scored 14 runs

**Above:** The great Ted Williams poses with his bat. Williams slugged 521 homers during his career, two of which came in the Red Sox's rout of the St. Louis Browns on June 8, 1950.

122

in the first inning, and the first 11 batters reached safely. Bill Mueller drove in six runs with four hits. Johnny Damon, Todd Walker, Manny Ramirez, and David Ortiz all knocked in three runs apiece. After joining the New York Yankees, Pavano got ripped again in a 17–1 loss to the Red Sox on May 28, 2005.

There was the 24–4 beating they handed to the Washington Senators on September 27, 1940, and the 23–3 bashing they gave the Tigers on June 18, 1953. On July 23, 2002, the Red Sox smoked Tampa Bay at Fenway 22–4 when Nomar Garciaparra knocked in eight runs with three homers, while Ramirez accounted for five runs with two homers and a double.

There was also a huge 20–6 rout of the Milwaukee Brewers on September 6, 1975, at County Stadium; Carlton Fisk led the charge with four RBI. And who can forget the 24–5 romp over the Cleveland Indians on August 21, 1986, when the Red Sox scored 12 runs in the sixth? Tony Armas led the way with six RBI and two homers while Dwight Evans and Marty Barrett also knocked in four apiece.

All in all, the Red Sox have scored 20 or more runs in 15 regular-season games.

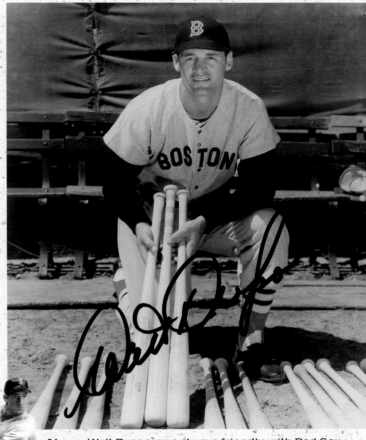

**Above:** Walt Dropo was always friendly with Red Sox fans. In the spring of 1989, he was guest at a New England sports collectors' club, where he talked about his winning the Rookie of the Year Award with the Red Sox and also signed photos, which he gave to each member—for free!
**Left:** Nomar Garciaparra action figures could be found in kids' rooms all across New England during his heyday with the Red Sox.

# Williams's Last At-Bat in 1960

**T**HE "SPLENDID SPLINTER"—42 and a little pudgy around the middle—treated it just like another at-bat and just another home run. Homer #521 in his final at-bat on September 28, 1960, against 21-year-old right-hander Jack Fisher of the Baltimore Orioles was anticlimactic. Just the way Williams wanted it.

Prior to the at-bat, Williams received a two-minute standing ovation from the 10,454 on hand at Fenway. That was after reading a three-sentence statement in an impromptu pregame ceremony.

After the home run, Williams received a second, heart-pounding ovation. He rounded the bases with his head down. He didn't tip his cap, and he didn't respond to several requests from the crowd for a curtain call.

In the top of the ninth, manager Mike Higgins made Williams go back to left. As soon as he took his position, Carroll Hardy replaced him. Williams made his final trot to the dugout. He again refused to tip his cap.

**Above:** A picture-perfect ending to a legendary career, Ted Williams crosses home plate after hitting a home run in the last at-bat of his career. He is congratulated by Jim Pagliaroni.
**Right:** Williams endorsed many products, including a soft drink that bore his name. The Moxie Company manufactured this drink, which came in bottles. Some featured Williams's picture and others just his first name.

# Rico Petrocelli Catches Final Pop-Up to Clinch the 1967 AL Pennant

DIEHARD RED SOX fans remember Ned Martin's call by heart: "The pitch . . . is looped toward shortstop, Petrocelli's back, he's got it. The Red Sox win, and it's pandemonium on the field."

It was the final out of the "Impossible Dream" regular season that October 1, 1967. The Red Sox beat the Twins 5–3 to clinch a tie for the American League pennant, which they won outright when the Tigers lost to the Angels in the second game of a double-header.

Petrocelli caught the final out off Rich Rollins's bat. "I just said, 'Don't drop it, please don't drop it,'" recalled Petrocelli. "It was a great day, a great time. We brought baseball back to Boston." Petrocelli was such a huge part of that team. Players said much later that he brought a certain toughness to the team. All great teams need an enforcer, and Petrocelli was certainly that.

Rico Petrocelli is a true-blue hometown favorite. During the 1967 Impossible Dream season, Petrocelli made a crucial defensive play in the last game of the regular season.

# Yaz Wins Triple Crown in 1967

CARL YASTRZEMSKI went after them: the American League pennant and the Triple Crown.

He went 7-for-8 in the final two games vs. the Twins, and he hit .417 (40-for-96) with 9 homers and 26 RBI from September 1 on, raising his average from .308 to .326. "You just get locked in," Yaz told *Globe* columnist Dan Shaughnessy in 2005. "Nothing bothers you at all. You don't hear the fans. You don't hear anything. You just have this tremendous focus. You think you're the only person in the ballpark."

How hot was Yaz? He ended August hitting .308 while Baltimore's Frank Robinson was hitting .331. When the regular season concluded, Yaz's .326 average was 15 points better than Robinson's. Yaz also had eight more RBI than the Twins' Harmon Killebrew.

The home run race was the most closely contested of the three categories. Yaz and Killebrew finished tied with 44. Both players hit homers on September 30, the next to last game of the season, for their 44th, but neither homered in the series finale on October 1.

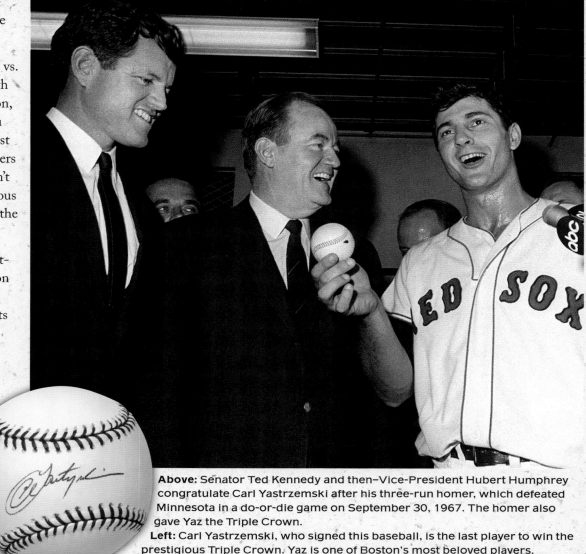

**Above:** Senator Ted Kennedy and then–Vice-President Hubert Humphrey congratulate Carl Yastrzemski after his three-run homer, which defeated Minnesota in a do-or-die game on September 30, 1967. The homer also gave Yaz the Triple Crown.
**Left:** Carl Yastrzemski, who signed this baseball, is the last player to win the prestigious Triple Crown. Yaz is one of Boston's most beloved players.

# Fisk's Game 6 12th-Inning Walk-Off in 1975 Series

Carlton Fisk hits a walk-off home run past the left-field foul pole during Game 6 of the 1975 World Series against the Reds. Fisk's blast evened the Series at three games apiece.

**I**T WAS 12:34 A.M., and more than five hours of baseball had been played, when Carlton Fisk shot from All-Star catcher to living legend with one swing of his bat.

This was the sixth game of the 1975 World Series, bottom of the 12th inning with the score knotted at 6. More than 35,000 fans waited breathlessly in the Fenway stands as Fisk led off the inning. After his stroke down the left-field line on Pat Darcy's pitch, Fisk stood at home plate and jumped up and down waving his arms as he tried to direct it fair. He succeeded. The ball sailed inside the foul pole, which the Red Sox later named the "Fisk Foul Pole." The Red Sox won Game 6 of the 1975 World Series over the Cincinnati Reds, 7–6, on Fisk's walk-off 12th-inning homer.

"This was the most emotional game I've ever played," Fisk told reporters after the celebration. "I will never forget this as long as I live." And he hasn't. Nor has any other Boston baseball fan.

# FREAKISH MOMENTS

IT WAS SEPTEMBER 7, 1935, at Fenway. Last of the ninth in the first game of a doubleheader. The Red Sox trailed 5–3, but they loaded the bases with nobody out. Joe Cronin's line drive hit Indians third baseman Odell Hale on the head and caromed to shortstop Bill Knickerbocker, who started a game-ending triple play.

A weird occurrence like this one undoubtedly stunned the Boston patrons. But many other strange events have given fans much to talk about. Bizarre in a different kind of

way was when St. Louis Browns hurler Ellis Kinder was about to throw a pitch from the Fenway mound. Just then a seagull flew by and dropped a three-pound fish next to him in a game on May 17, 1945.

Old-time Red Sox fans also recall a June 11, 1962, game against Cleveland. The Indians had the bases loaded in the third inning. Red Sox pitcher Earl Wilson was about to throw the ball when a voice cried, "Hold it, Earl!" Wilson stumbled off the mound and was called for a balk. The voice was that

Joe Cronin was a seven-time All-Star shortstop, who knocked in more than 1,400 runs during his Hall-of-Fame career. Unfortunately, for the Fenway fans who attended the September 7, 1935, doubleheader, none of his RBI came in the final inning of the first game.

of Tito Francona, who was the Indians runner at first. The Tribe wound up winning 10–0.

Boston first baseman Dick Stuart was known as "Dr. Strangeglove" for his poor fielding, but on August 19, 1963, at Fenway, Stuart hit an inside-the-park homer off the Green Monster. Cleveland Indian center-fielder Vic Davalillo and left-fielder John Romano collided, the ball rolling away into the left-field corner. Stuart was really slow, but the circumstances allowed him to score.

During the Impossible Dream 1967 run, Red Sox reliever John Wyatt was hit in the head on a throw from catcher Bob Tillman, who was trying to gun down Al Kaline stealing second. The Red Sox eventually lost the game 5–4.

And who can forget April 25, 1990, when Angels out-fielder Claudell Washington hit the right-field wall at Fenway while chasing Bill Buckner's drive to the corner? His momentum carried him over the fence, and he got stuck in the first row of seating. Buckner, who could barely run because of his injured ankles and knees, was able to come home on the only inside-the-park homer of his career.

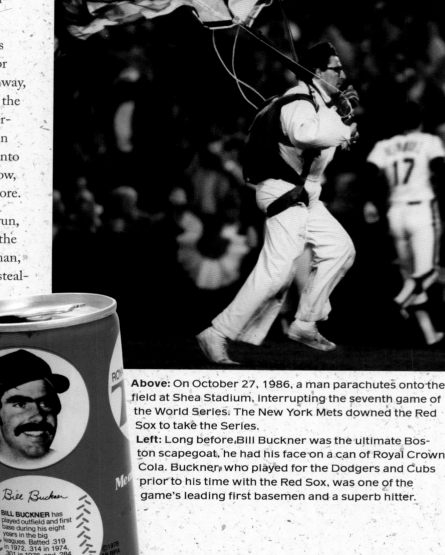

**Above:** On October 27, 1986, a man parachutes onto the field at Shea Stadium, interrupting the seventh game of the World Series. The New York Mets downed the Red Sox to take the Series.
**Left:** Long before Bill Buckner was the ultimate Boston scapegoat, he had his face on a can of Royal Crown Cola. Buckner, who played for the Dodgers and Cubs prior to his time with the Red Sox, was one of the game's leading first basemen and a superb hitter.

BILL BUCKNER has played outfield and first base during his eight years in the big leagues. Batted .319 in 1972, .314 in 1974, .301 in 1976, and .284 in 1977. Played in one championship series.
No. 70 of 100

RC Collector's Series No. Two

# Roger Clemens Strikes Out 20 Mariners in 1986

DURING SOME IDLE chatter with Red Sox pitcher Al Nipper prior to the April 29, 1986, game against Seattle at Fenway, Red Sox first baseman Bill Buckner predicted, "Roger's gonna strike out 18 tonight." Buckner was off by two. He anticipated a high strikeout game because the Mariners had been whiffed 166 times in their first 19 games, more than any other team in the American League to that point. And Clemens, of course, was dealing.

"The way he's been throwing and the way they've been striking out, 18 seemed like the number," admitted Buckner to reporters after the game.

At one point Clemens struck out eight straight batters. Fans who normally put up "K" cards on the back of the center-field bleachers for each Clemens's strikeout were running out of cards and space. In the ninth, he struck out Spike Owen swinging and Phil Bradley whiffed on three pitches for No. 20, making Clemens the first pitcher in almost 150,000 major-league games to punch out 20. Clemens and the Red Sox won the game 3–1 thanks to a two-out, three-run, seventh-inning homer by Dwight Evans, which got lost in the hoopla.

One side note: Clemens was apprised that he was going for the record by Nipper before he took the mound in the ninth. "I had to," Nipper said. "I think you should know if you're going for something like that. What if you didn't know and you didn't get it because you didn't know?"

**Below:** Roger Clemens poses with a signed 20K ball from 1986. He had fanned 20 Mariners before the Red Sox faithful at Fenway Park.
**Bottom Right:** Every sports card collector knows that this Clemens card from the 1984 Fleer update set is considered his extra-rookie card. And because of its rarity, it is highly desirable.

FLEER

Roger Clemens
PITCHER

# Dave Henderson Saves the Playoffs in 1986

THE LATE HAYWOOD Sullivan, a co-owner of the team along with Jean Yawkey, got quite a chuckle when he learned that Dave Henderson spoiled the Angels' party on that October 12, 1986, day at Anaheim Stadium. Literally. "Some of the clubhouse employees were already popping champagne in the clubhouse prior to the start of the ninth inning," Sullivan said.

One pitch away from elimination, "Hendu" blasted a 2–2 forkball from Donnie Moore into the left-center field bleachers to give the Red Sox a 6–5 lead, bringing a collective hush to one of the noisiest playoff venues in history. The game went 11 innings before Henderson's bases-loaded sacrifice fly sent the series back to Boston, where the Red Sox won two games to win the AL Championship Series in seven.

"I had waited my entire career for a moment like that," said Henderson. "When I played in Seattle, we'd be out of the race and watching the playoffs at home. It was a great moment for all of us because everyone had us dead."

"Hendu" was an integral part of the Red Sox' 1986 storybook season. Acquired in midseason, Dave Henderson (pointing his finger upward while running with Rich Gedman) paid dividends as he kept the Red Sox alive with a dramatic ninth-inning home run in Game 5 of the ALCS against the California Angels.

# "Morgan's Magic" Produces 19 Wins Out of 20 After the 1988 All-Star Break

"**W**ALPOLE" JOE MORGAN was a local guy who used to plow snow on the Massachusetts Turnpike. He was a coach on manager John McNamara's staff. In 1988, the Red Sox were having a dismal and lackluster first half, which forced Red Sox ownership to fire McNamara at the All-Star break and hire Morgan on an interim basis. "My job is to get faith into this ballclub," Morgan said the day he was hired.

Morgan's club won 19 of their first 20 games under his helm. Morgan made one big change—Jody Reed became his shortstop and Spike Owen was benched. On the first day Morgan managed, the Red Sox swept a doubleheader from the Royals. Kevin Romine won a game 7–6 with his first major-league homer after the Red Sox had trailed by a 6–0 score. Todd Benzinger won a game against Minnesota on a memorable homer in the bottom of the tenth. On that day, July 20, Morgan had the interim label removed.

Morgan's Red Sox lost for the first time on July 26 after winning 12 straight in a 9–8 loss to the Texas Rangers. But Morgan's squad won seven straight after that. At the end of the month, Morgan's Red Sox were 17 games over .500 and 1½ games off the AL East lead. Boston wound up winning its division.

"It was magic," recalled Reed many years later. "He was the right manager at the right time."

The Red Sox were struggling in 1988 when the team promoted Joe Morgan to manager. Boston then won 12 games in a row and 19 of 20 to surge from fourth place to a division title. The wild run was known as "Morgan's Magic."

# Roger Clemens Strikes Out 20 Tigers in 1996

**I**N HIS FINAL WIN in a Red Sox uniform, you might say Roger Clemens got the whole enchilada. He struck out 20 Detroit Tigers in a 4–0 shutout before only 8,779 at Tiger Stadium on September 18, 1996, his second 20-strikeout performance in ten years. In the process, he tied a team record held by Cy Young for most wins (192) and shutouts (38).

"You never expect to strike out 20 batters," said Clemens, who was extremely emotional that night sensing he was near the end of his Red Sox career. "I'm so blessed to have done this twice in my career."

Clemens threw 151 pitches, struck out the side three times, and allowed five hits. And just like his first 20-strikeout game, he didn't walk a batter. The game was significant for Clemens, who was showing his dominance again after three seasons of decline due to injuries.

Clemens left the team following the season and signed a free-agent deal with the Toronto Blue Jays.

**Right:** Clemens repeats his April 29, 1986, record-setting, strikeout performance. It is now ten years later, and he whiffs 20 at Tiger Stadium on September 18, 1996.
**Above:** A baseball signed by seven-time Cy Young Award-winning pitcher Roger Clemens is a true collector's item.

# COLOR US RED SOX

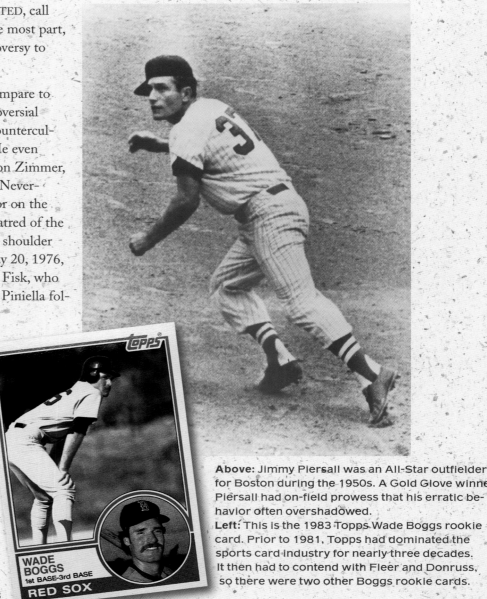

OLORFUL, CRAZY, OPINIONATED, call them what you want. For the most part, they added spice, fun, and controversy to Red Sox lore.

What baseball player could compare to Bill "Spaceman" Lee? The controversial left-hander was known for his counterculture philosophies and lifestyle. He even nicknamed Red Sox manager Don Zimmer, whom he feuded with, "Gerbil." Nevertheless, he was a fierce competitor on the mound and was known for his hatred of the rival Yankees. He injured his left shoulder in a bench-clearing brawl on May 20, 1976, when he tried to defend Carlton Fisk, who was engaged in a fight with Lou Piniella following a home-plate collision.

Another notable player is former Red Sox center-fielder Carl Everett, who publicly denied that dinosaurs had ever existed. Like Lee, Everett could be volatile. In 2000, he received a 10-game suspension for butting noses with umpire Ron Kulpa, who said Everett was using an illegal batting stance.

Hall of Fame third baseman Wade Boggs was so superstitious

WADE BOGGS
1st BASE-3rd BASE
RED SOX

**Above:** Jimmy Piersall was an All-Star outfielder for Boston during the 1950s. A Gold Glove winner, Piersall had on-field prowess that his erratic behavior often overshadowed.
**Left:** This is the 1983 Topps Wade Boggs rookie card. Prior to 1981, Topps had dominated the sports card industry for nearly three decades. It then had to contend with Fleer and Donruss, so there were two other Boggs rookie cards.

that he ate chicken before every game. That's why Jim Rice called him the "chicken man." In 1984, Boggs and his wife, Debbie, authored a cookbook entitled *Fowl Tips*.

There were players with a language of their own. Talented defensive first baseman George Scott called home runs "taters." Dennis Eckersley referred to a fastball as "cheese" and a curveball as a "yakker."

One of the more troubled Red Sox was Dennis "Oil Can" Boyd, who earned his nickname during his beer-drinking days in his hometown of Meridian, Mississippi, where beer was called "oil." Boyd fought personal demons and battled the effects of the racism he had endured in his childhood. In 1986, he went ballistic when he learned that he was left off the American League All-Star team. Later that year, he cried uncontrollably after he was told Bruce Hurst was replacing him as the World Series Game 7 starter.

But certainly the most out-of-control was Jimmy Piersall, who suffered a nervous breakdown after a series of events from May through June 1952. He then had a long stay at the Westborough Mental Hospital in Massachusetts. Piersall's breakdown led to his book *Fear Strikes Out*.

"I'm crazy and I got the papers to prove it," he said in many interviews. In a later book, he commented, "The crackup was probably the best thing that ever happened to me. Whoever heard of Jimmy Piersall before that happened?"

But Piersall was also a colorful character on other clubs. Upon hitting his 100th career homer in 1963 with the New York Mets, Piersall ran the bases backward.

**Right:** The NESN cameras have a knack for capturing the hilarity that ensues from time to time inside the Red Sox dugout. In 1999, teammates tied Pedro Martinez to a dugout pole with tape. Not to worry—Pedro was always good at getting out of sticky situations.

# Ted Williams Tribute at the 1999 All-Star Game in Boston

HE WAS 80 YEARS OLD and had been driven out to the Fenway pitcher's mound in a golf cart. Announced as "the greatest hitter who ever lived," Williams listened as the crowd roared.

Encircled by 31 of the greatest ballplayers of all time and All-Stars from the American and National Leagues, Williams laughed and cried. Willie Mays, Stan Musial, Bob Feller, Cal Ripken, Jr., and Bob Gibson were among those who stood around him. They shared stories and posed for pictures as cameras flashed from all directions.

"It was like something out of *Field of Dreams*," said Jim Thome, who was on the American League roster as a Cleveland Indian. As Mark McGwire and Tony Gwynn stood on either side of him, Carlton Fisk received the "first pitch" of the All-Star Game from Williams, and the crowd went wild.

The game was supposed to start and players were asked to leave the field, but nobody did.

The 1999 All-Star Game at Fenway Park was rich in baseball history. Prior to the first pitch, Major League Baseball and the Boston Red Sox organized a tribute to Ted Williams in the infield. Williams was surrounded by members of the All-Century Team, and the 1999 All-Stars paid their respects to the greatest hitter who ever lived.

# Pedro Martinez's All-Star Show in 1999

FOLLOWING AN EMOTIONALLY draining tribute to Ted Williams in one of the most heart-wrenching pregame festivities in All-Star Game history at Fenway Park on July 13, 1999, Pedro Martinez continued the party. He struck out the side in the first and had two more Ks in the second.

"This is probably more than I expected," said Martinez after being crowned the All-Star Game MVP. "I just wanted to be a part of it, have fun with it. I thought seeing Ted Williams come in and the crowd going wild and the planes passing by, this one we'll hopefully all enjoy, the fans and me."

Martinez struck out Barry Larkin, Larry Walker, and Sammy Sosa in the first inning and Mark McGwire and Jeff Bagwell in the second. The *Globe*'s Gordon Edes likened it to Carl Hubbell of the Giants striking out Babe Ruth, Lou Gehrig, Jimmie Foxx, Al Simmons, and Joe Cronin in succession 65 years earlier.

**Above:** Boston's Pedro Martinez pitches in the first inning of the 1999 All-Star Game. Fenway Park hosted this baseball classic. **Left:** Bobblehead dolls have become popular in recent years. Red Sox fans can collect all their favorites including this Pedro Martinez bobblehead. Pedro is truly one of a kind.

# RED SOX CONTROVERSY

# WILLIAMS vs. ORTIZ

**W**HEN RED SOX general manager Theo Epstein acquired David Ortiz at the start of the 2003 season, few baseball experts could foresee the impact Ortiz would make on the sport. "Big Papi" has become the league's poster child for clutch hitting and big home runs. During the 2004 postseason, Ortiz put together perhaps the greatest clutch-hitting run in Red Sox history. It began in Game 3 of the ALDS against the Angels. In the bottom of the 10th inning, Ortiz sent a moon shot over the Green Monster to ensure the first-round sweep.

His clutch run continued in the ALCS against the hated New York Yankees. Facing a Game 4 elimination, Ortiz hit a 12th-inning bomb into the right-field seats to keep the Red Sox playoff hopes alive. Then, during Game 5 Papi struck again, this time with a well-placed single in the 14th inning of the longest playoff game in baseball history. It brought the Red Sox back into a series they would amazingly win.

With countless game-winning and walk-off homers on his resume, Papi has ignited Red Sox Nation like no other player. The only question now is: Do we appreciate it enough? For when Ortiz steps up to bat with

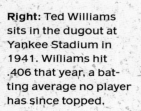

**Right:** Ted Williams sits in the dugout at Yankee Stadium in 1941. Williams hit .406 that year, a batting average no player has since topped.

The Boston Globe

Playoffs04

**David, goliath**

Sportsplus

**Swing king**

Playoffs04

**Marathon man**

# MR. CLUTCH
The Greatest Clutch Hitter in the History of Boston Baseball

**Right:** The legend of David Ortiz reached new heights during the 2004 ALCS. He followed up his Game 4 walk-off home run with a Game 5 walk-off single in the 14th inning, single-handedly sending the series back to the Bronx.

**Top Right:** David Ortiz has earned the nickname "Mr. Clutch." "Big Papi" is one of New England's most beloved sports stars, and his Mr. Clutch poster is available at souvenir stores.

the game on the line, Red Sox fans don't hope for magic, they expect it.

Now, compare Ortiz to Ted Williams, the standard-bearer of greatness for a previous generation of Red Sox Nation. His toughness unmatched, Williams's flare for the dramatic has left old-timers telling stories to their kids and grandkids for decades. Evidence of this is in the 1941 All-Star Game. In one of the most memorable All-Star Games of all time, the American League found themselves down 5–4 in the bottom of the ninth inning. With two men aboard, Teddy Ballgame launched a walk-off homer into the right-field stands to give the AL a 7–5 victory.

We turn to one of Williams's former teammates, Dominic DiMaggio, to settle the score: Williams or Ortiz in the clutch?

"I love watching Ortiz as a fan," DiMaggio said. "He's had a couple of unbelievable years. He's got that swagger, creates drama, but I can't erase 19 years of what Ted Williams did so many times for so many years."

# Dave Roberts Steals Second in Game 4 in 2004 ALCS

Facing elimination in Game 4 of the 2004 ALCS, the Fenway faithful prayed for a miracle, and they got it in the form of Dave Roberts's stolen base. "The Steal" led the rally against super-closer Mariano Rivera and started the ultimate three-games-to-none comeback against the Yankees.

ENOS SLAUGHTER is known for his "mad dash" from first to home in the 1946 World Series against the Red Sox, but in the 2004 playoffs, Red Sox center fielder Dave Roberts made the most memorable dash in Red Sox history.

In Game 4 of the American League Championship Series against the Yankees, the Red Sox were on the brink of being swept, down 4–3. Pinch-running for Kevin Millar, who had drawn a walk in the bottom of the ninth, Roberts changed the course of history. Roberts took off from first on Mariano Rivera's first pitch to Bill Mueller. Jorge Posada threw down to Derek Jeter covering second. Safe! Mueller then drove in Roberts to tie the game. The Red Sox won that game and the next three games to capture the AL pennant.

"Everybody knew what I was going to do," recalled Roberts. "It was nerve-wracking, but that was my job. It's one thing to do the unexpected, but it's tougher when . . . people know you're going to try it."

# Curt Schilling and His Bloody Sock

**Above:** Curt Schilling fires from the mound in Game 2 of the 2004 World Series. Schilling officially reached hero status in Red Sox Nation with a 2004 postseason for the ages.

**Left:** Here is a baseball autographed by Red Sox ace Curt Schilling. Schilling has pitched his way into the hearts and minds of Red Sox fans since his arrival in 2004.

**R**ED SOX GENERAL MANAGER Theo Epstein probably said it best: "I'm convinced that ten years from now people are going to say [gimpy-legged New York Knicks hero] Willis Reed pulled a Curt Schilling, instead of the other way around." No doubt, Schilling's gutsy performance in Game 6 against the Yankees to tie the American League Championship Series at 3–3 saved the day for the Red Sox.

Just a couple of days before, Dr. William Morgan had performed a creative surgical procedure in which he sutured the dislocated tendon in Schilling's right ankle to his skin. Blood stained the sock on his right foot early in the game, but Schilling persevered for 99 pitches and held a 4–1 lead before finally leaving the game in the seventh.

Before the game, Schilling threw on the side. The plan was that if he could, he'd pitch to a couple of batters in relief. But Schilling stepped up and said, "There's no game tomorrow. It's all about right now. It can be done. I could do it." And he did!

# The Red Sox Are Champions—Again!

ON THAT EARLY OCTOBER 29 morning, champagne dripped down his hair into his face after winning the clinching Game 4 of the 2007 World Series against Colorado. A year earlier, lefty Jon Lester was bracing for chemotherapy treatments to treat his cancer. "I couldn't have asked for more than this," Lester said of his Game 4 win at Coors Field. "I couldn't have prayed for anything more. This is a dream come true. Everything that I've gone through—and now this."

The '07 Red Sox, who won 96 games and tied the Indians for most wins in the majors, led the American League East from April 18 on. Their dominance was reflected with a 12-game lead on July 5. They had a horse, 20-game winner Josh Beckett, and they rode him for key wins leading to a sweep of the Los Angeles Angels in the Divisional Series, and a key Game 5 win at Jacobs Field enabled the Sox to come back from a 3–1 deficit to the Cleveland Indians in the American League Championship Series to win two games at Fenway. Like in '04 when Boston swept the Cardinals, the Sox swept the Rockies to win their second 21st-century championship.

Red Sox pitching, second in the majors with a 3.87 ERA, thrived with Beckett; Japanese phenom Daisuke Matsuzaka, who won 15; 17-game winner Tim Wakefield; and the tremendous dominance of closer Jonathan Papelbon, who saved three of the four World Series wins.

The talented lineup featured AL Rookie of the Year second baseman Dustin Pedroia, a powerful middle order of David Ortiz, Manny Ramirez, and Mike Lowell, and a gritty Kevin Youkilis. When the Sox needed late energy, they got it from rookie center fielder Jacoby Ellsbury, who hit .438 in the World Series (and doubled twice in the same inning in Game 3).

The Bambino's curse ended in 2004; now it's completely forgotten.

**Above:** Josh Beckett was virtually unhittable in the 2007 postseason, going 4–0 and allowing only four earned runs in 30 innings after a 20–7 regular season.
**Top right:** This Red Sox 2007 World Series program is a popular item in Boston.
**Opposite Page:** After striking out Colorado's Seth Smith for the final out of the clinching Game 4 of the 2007 World Series, Jonathan Papelbon is engulfed by teammates in celebration of Boston's second world championship in four years at Coors Field.

# Index